01 14

A Rome
for Restless
Hearts

A Rome
for Restless
Hearts

FINDING A SPIRITUAL HOME IN CATHOLICISM

Sister Lisa Hezmalhalch

IMAGE

NEW YORK

Image
An imprint of the Penguin Random House Christian Publishing Group,
a division of Penguin Random House LLC
1745 Broadway
New York, NY 10019

imagecatholicbooks.com
penguinrandomhouse.com

Hardcover ISBN 978-0-593-72839-0
Ebook ISBN 978-0-593-72840-6

Printed in the United States of America on acid-free paper

2 4 6 8 9 7 5 3 1

First Edition

The authorized representative in the EU for product safety and compliance is
Penguin Random House Ireland, Morrison Chambers, 32 Nassau Street,
Dublin D02 YH68, Ireland. https://eu-contact.penguin.ie

BOOK TEAM: Production editor: Jennifer Rodriguez •
Managing editor: Sally Franklin • Production manager: Meghan O'Leary •
Copy editor: Lawrence Krauser • Proofreaders: Debbie Anderson,
Andrea Gordon, Lisa Nicholas

Book design by Caroline Cunningham

For details on special quality discounts for bulk purchases,
contact specialmarketscms@penguinrandomhouse.com

To God the Father,

the Author of all my Adventures,

Jesus, my Savior and constant companion,

the Holy Spirit, my Counselor and source of Truth,

and Mary for teaching me to keep my hands open to

what God has in store.

CONTENTS

CONTENTS

An Average Day in a Not-So-Average Life

The most common question people have when they find out I'm a religious sister is "What does your daily schedule look like?" and I have to remind myself that my life no longer looks like the life most people live.

I used to do whatever I wanted with my time. I mean, I had a job that dictated about forty hours of my week, but outside of that I was free—free to travel and visit friends in exotic places, free to binge-watch hours of *Doctor Who,* free to sleep in, free to go out to eat, to go antique shopping, redecorate my house, get a pet, or do nothing at all.

That used to be my life. And instead of using my freedom of choice to continue doing all that, I chose to live my life by the ringing of bells.

Ding-a-ling! Ding-a-ling! Ding-a-ling!

It's 5:50 A.M. on a Sunday morning and the prayer bell is letting me know that I have ten minutes to finish what

I'm doing and get to morning prayer. Out of habit, I grab a few items off the desk in my room, loading up my pockets with keys, ChapStick, a handkerchief, and a rosary. Then I kiss my large crucifix necklace, putting the cord over my head and hiding the crucifix underneath my habit. I wear the same thing every day, so getting ready requires little thought, giving me more time for reflection and prayer as I begin my day.

The life of a religious sister is built around a daily schedule of prayers, which begin at 6:00 A.M. and continue in intervals throughout the day. By the time I crawl back into bed, I've paused my life to pray at least eight times.

The chapel is quiet except for the sound of the overhead fan. When it's summer, there's sunlight that comes through the large window behind the altar and tabernacle, warming the room with the Arizona sun.

The quiet ring of another bell signals it's time to stand and begin prayer. The silence I've kept since the close of prayer the night before is broken as I begin to chant the psalms. Morning prayer, also known as lauds, is followed immediately by prime. These make up the first two prayers of the day and will take about thirty-five to forty minutes to complete.

This leaves plenty of time for a simple breakfast after prayer. Breakfast is the only meal of the day that is optional, and therefore it's the one you make yourself. After a cup of coffee and a couple of scrambled eggs from our community's farm, I wash my dishes and finish getting ready for the day.

This particular morning, I'm making a breakfast casserole to bring to our fellowship potluck after Sunday Mass in a couple of hours. Once I've put it in the oven and washed the dishes, I have a little bit more time to prepare some food donations to be canned. This week we got a couple pounds of pickling cucumbers that are on the verge of going bad. So I sweep in to save the day by whipping up a quick pickling brine and cutting up the good parts of the cucumbers to be canned. The parts that have already spoiled are stored in a Tupperware container. Those scraps will be used by the brothers to feed the pigs and chickens.

It's 8:50 A.M. and the prayer bell is ringing again. I have ten minutes to get to prayer. Since Sundays are busy with mass and fellowship afterward, the prayers of terce and sext, prayed at 10:00 A.M. and noon, respectively, are joined together and prayed at 9:00 A.M. When I finish at 9:20 A.M., I load up the casserole and take it over to the parish hall and set up for fellowship.

At 10:45 A.M., it's time to head over to the church. I scan the small crowd to see if any of my usual volunteers are there so I can call on them to read the Scripture during Mass. Summer in the White Mountains of Arizona usually means many of our parishioners, especially the older and retired ones, travel to see their kids and grandkids. If they're gone, I become the default reader during Mass. Sure enough, I see that my usual folks aren't around, so I pick up the missalette—a book with all the Mass readings in it—and scan the readings of the day just in case there are any challenging words I need to practice beforehand.

Mass ends around noon, and about half of the parishioners from Mass head with me over to the hall. After we all have our fill of the potluck-style brunch, it's time to clean up. By 1:30 P.M., I'm back at the convent. My first task is to put away the leftover casserole as well as some of the other food that people sent with me. There's a lot of leftover watermelon that I'll be bringing to share with the brothers for dinner.

I then spend the next hour or so focusing on my online ministry on TikTok. First I check for any private messages asking for prayer. There's one from a follower in Australia asking me to pray for a family member. After I've said a prayer for them, I check the latest video comments: Someone is asking for an update on the new community. With the time I have left I decide to work on recording a video in response to their request.

Ding-a-ling! Ding-a-ling! Ding-a-ling!

It's 2:50 P.M. and time to pray nones. With that ten-minute prayer finished, I pack up the food scraps I've been saving for the pigs all week (along with the extra watermelon), hop in the car, and drive twenty minutes to the next town, where our community farm is located, as well as the brothers who run it.

I get there in time to hear another bell: *Ding-dong! Ding-dong! Ding-dong!*

Our community Holy Hour is from 4:00 P.M. to 5:00 P.M., followed by vespers, also known as evening prayer, then dinner. Tonight, Brother Eric is making homemade chicken potpie along with a salad of veggies from the brothers' garden; and, of course, we'll have the leftover watermelon.

We're a small community, consisting of four brothers and myself, the only sister. While we'll see each other off and on during the week, Sunday nights are our main evening to relax and catch up. Tonight after dinner, we decide to play a game, Throw Throw Burrito, while we enjoy a cheesecake one of the locals made for us.

Ding-a-ling! Ding-a-ling! Ding-a-ling!

It's 8:50 P.M. and the bells let me know that it's time to get home to pray the last prayers of the day. Matins and compline, also known as the office of readings and night prayer, complete our day. Once we finish praying compline, we practice what's known as the grand silence. We won't speak again until prayer the next morning.

Sometimes it feels like people think religious brothers, sisters, and nuns are just sort of born living like this, but I can assure you I certainly was not. Not only did I used to do whatever I wanted with my time—I wasn't even Catholic. In fact, I didn't even think Catholics were Christians at all. Catholicism was just some weird spin-off cult to be avoided at all costs.

Yet here I am living my life as a Catholic sister by the ringing of the bells, and loving every minute of it.

THE ADVENTURE

The voyage of discovery lies not in finding new land-
scapes, but in having new eyes.

—MARCEL PROUST

In June 2015, I bought a journal to keep track of a new adventure. I had spent the first thirty-four years of my life as a devout and on-fire Protestant Christian. I had always dreamed of doing big things for the Lord: I was willing to go anywhere and do anything to serve Jesus, and to help others grow in their faith. But I never suspected that the Lord would invite me on this voyage that, as Proust so astutely observed in the quotation above, would require me to see everything anew—this voyage to Catholicism, Tik-Tok fame, and a life of founding a new religious order of Catholic nuns.

For me, growing up, Catholicism was an unknown that existed in the background religious landscape. My stepdad was raised Catholic, and his parents still practiced their Catholic faith, but my interactions with them were infrequent, and what little of their faith I saw didn't seem to be anything more than images of Jesus, Mary, and the saints. When I was twelve, I toured Catholic cathedrals in France. While their beauty was astounding, I saw them as extravagant wastes of money that could have been used to help those in need. From my perspective, Catholics didn't love Jesus as much as they loved rituals, rules, and rosaries. The only good Catholic experience I had was watching the *Sister Act* movies, but as much as I loved those singing nuns, I came away with the impression that nuns were so set in their ways, they needed an outsider to come in and wake them up.

I had no interest in the Catholic Church, but I loved the Christian faith I knew! From childhood, Jesus was my everything. I attended church every chance I got, soaked up Sunday School lessons, attended vacation Bible schools, Awana,* camps, and mission trips. I volunteered in different ministries at church, served food to the homeless, delivered Christmas gifts to needy kids, and even sang in the choir at a Billy Graham crusade. All the while I was reading my Bible, praying to Jesus, and striving to live a life of love and service. I was in love with Jesus and obsessed with my faith. I even got a full-time job as a janitor at my church! I was over the moon; I was getting paid to serve the Lord!

So it's no surprise that I chose a college where everyone majored in Bible and theology. My desire to help others led me to a master's degree in pastoral care. I had no idea what the future held, but I knew that with this new degree I'd be even more prepared to serve God and to help others grow in their faith.

During my graduate studies, a friend of mine became Catholic. I was horrified! By this point I saw Catholicism as

---

* Awana is a Bible club designed to help students memorize portions of Scripture and learn about the Christian faith.

a perversion of the Christian faith that led people on an easy road to life apart from God—hell. I was worried for my friend's soul. I tackled each issue I had with the Catholic Church, doing research, reading Scripture, asking questions, and constantly praying.

After all that investigation, I came to realize that the ideas I'd had about Catholicism were plain wrong. I no longer had major issues with someone else choosing to be Catholic—but I still wasn't interested in Catholicism for myself.

But the Lord had other plans. In my final semester of graduate school, I felt the Lord quietly tap me on the shoulder and let me know: He was indeed calling me to become Catholic. As I perused the shelves at a local bookstore, looking for a journal, I saw one with the Proust quotation on it. I'd found the blank slate I needed to document my discoveries. I had no idea what lay ahead, but with Jesus firmly grasping my hand, I knew He would lead me where He wanted me to go.

RELIGIOUS LIFE AND TIKTOK

I downloaded TikTok in the spring of 2020, at the start of the Covid-19 outbreak while living in northern California. It could help me connect with the outside world while we were all in quarantine, I figured, and at the very least make me laugh a little. At that point, I had only been Catholic for four years and wasn't a nun yet. But that adventure was waiting just around the corner. I wondered if perhaps religious life—that is, living as a Catholic nun—was part of God's plan for me.

I'd been exploring different religious orders (the general term used for groups of sisters and nuns) since I'd become Catholic, and had even talked with a group of seminarians (men studying to be priests) about starting a new one. But when Covid-19 hit pause on the world, I had to trust the Lord. If He was leading me into religious life, He'd show me when and how. Not so long afterward, my seminarian friends let me know they were leaving the seminary and entering an existing men's religious order of priests and brothers in southern California, and that their order was interested in founding a women's religious order to mirror their own. I had asked the Lord to show me when and how, and apparently His answer was *now*—during a global pandemic.

It was truly invigorating, learning what it meant to be a Catholic sister and how to found a new religious order of sisters. Because everyone was quarantined in their homes, we had lots of time to pray, study, and learn; but our interactions with folks were severely limited. When the community heard me talk about how people were using TikTok to stay connected with the rest of humanity, they suggested I start posting videos as well. My meager following grew as I posted videos about movies I'd watched, meals I was making for the community, and a few funny trends.

It was when I started answering questions about religious life that my engagement soared: I discovered just how many people were hungry to learn about this mysterious and ancient tradition. The thing that surprised me was how many Catholics, Protestants, Jews, agnostics, pagans, witches, atheists, former Catholics, and everyone in between had questions. I was limited in my in-person interactions, but thanks to a little phone app I quickly found myself engaging with over 140,000 people from all over the world and all walks of life.

People sent me letters and messages with prayer requests and questions about life and faith. One asked me how it felt to know that there was a group of people in the world now that considered me "a bit of a celebrity." The weight of responsibility grew as several people recounted bad experiences with the Catholic Church, or with nuns. I was sobered by the realization that, as an imperfect human, I could either help or hinder the faith of those who watched me. The potential to do good was amazing; the potential to harm was terrifying.

After about a year, the seminarians-turned-brothers and I left the established community we had joined: we still felt called to establish a new religious order. We followed the Lord to Arizona and, to my surprise, my TikTok community followed along for the ride. The commenters were curious about the new order, our growing farm, daily life, and my work in the Church and the local Catholic school. After mentioning in a few videos that I hadn't always been Catholic, I began getting questions about that journey: How could I go from being a Protestant to becoming a Catholic nun?

So many people connected with those videos in which I talked about my journey into the Catholic Church, but I needed a format that didn't confine me to a few minutes at a time, and that would allow me to explain more thoroughly the doubt, confusion, joy, peace, and overall paradigm shift that one experiences in having new eyes. Hence, this book!

INTO THE UNKNOWN

This book is an invitation: for you to embark on a journey, to look at your faith with new eyes. This opportunity may intrigue you or terrify you—or both! My own journey required me to look for God beyond the safe confines I'd kept Him in all my life. It required a huge paradigm shift that caused real emotional vertigo. But what is a leap of faith without fear, risk, and hope?

"I'm afraid of what I'm risking if I follow you / Into the unknown." When I first heard this lyric in the song "Into the Unknown" from *Frozen II,* all I could think about was how I felt taking that leap of faith the Lord asked of me. But what encouraged me was the beauty I saw along the way, the positive growth I experienced, the love for Jesus that grew deeper—and the deeper love I discovered He had for me.

My goal in this book is to help you bravely take your own leap of faith into whatever the Lord is calling you to. Your leap may be talking to Him for the first time, or the first time in a while. Your leap may be to ask more questions about the faith you've always had, or a faith you've long since rejected. Your leap may seem simple to some, but terrifying to you. No matter what your leap is, I hope there is something in my journey that may encourage you in your own.

A Rome

for Restless

Hearts

CHAPTER 1

Who Is Jesus?

I love You, beloved Jesus; I love You more than I love myself. With all my heart I repent of ever having offended You. Grant that I may love You always; and then do with me as You will.

—SAINT ALPHONSUS LIGUORI

FIRST IMPRESSIONS

When I was about eight years old, I was in a Bible club called Awana. We met weekly, played games, and heard Bible stories. Much like Boy Scouts and Girl Scouts, in Awana you received little merit badges and moved up in rank when you completed tasks like attending meetings, memorizing Bible verses, or reciting Christian teachings.

On one occasion I was on the verge of earning my next achievement award and only had one verse left to memorize. I read that verse over and over again, trying to get those ancient words to stick. For some reason, this one was more challenging than all the other verses I had memorized. Try as I might, I couldn't seem to get any of those words to stay in my head. Every time I'd ask my mom to quiz me, I'd forget words and even whole sections.

The day of our next Awana meeting was quickly approaching, and I didn't seem any closer to having that verse memorized than when I had begun! Frantically I asked my mom if she had any advice. She suggested I pray about it. She said that since the verse was about Jesus, He might want to help me remember what it says. I hadn't considered asking for Jesus's help, but what she said made sense.

So the night before my next Awana meeting I decided to give prayer a try. As I lay in bed, I asked Jesus for help to memorize this verse. I told Him how hard I'd worked and how much I wanted to move forward in the group. I ended the whole prayer with a little "Amen" as I dozed off to sleep.

That night, I had a simple yet profound dream. I couldn't see anything, but I heard a man's voice reciting the verse I'd been working so hard to memorize. What made this dream so indelible was how I felt at the sound of this man's voice. I felt safe, at peace, comforted, loved, seen, and excited. Even those words can't fully describe the feeling brought by that voice. And though I couldn't see anything, and I'd never heard that voice before, I knew Jesus was the one speaking.

As quickly as the dream began, once the verse had been recited the dream ended. I woke up the next morning and knew the verse by heart! I was so excited! Jesus had heard my tiny little prayer and helped me out!

Through the years, the verse ended up fading from my mind so much that I can no longer tell you what it said, but I have never forgotten that voice. I've walked through many seasons where I've wavered in my faith and wrestled with doubts: *Is God real? Did Jesus really exist? Do I actually believe any of this?* Each time I crept close to giving up on my faith, the memory of that dream would come back to me like a lifeline, pulling me out of a sea of doubt and reminding me of the tangible reality of that voice and the existence of the one who spoke.

MY BEST FRIEND/SAVIOR

I'd been taught by my family, Bible clubs, camps, vacation Bible schools, and the churches I attended that Jesus was the Son of God who came down from heaven, lived a holy life, taught divine wisdom, performed miracles, and was condemned to death on a cross to save us from our sins. He rose from the dead three days later, and then forty days after that ascended into heaven. I was also taught that He would return again at some unknown moment to judge all humanity.

The way I was raised to engage with Jesus was to ask Him to be my personal savior, ask His forgiveness when I sinned, and talk to Him as often as possible. I was encouraged by pastors, youth pastors, and Sunday School teachers to read the Bible daily in order to learn more about Jesus.

I did all this and more. When I was a little girl I would lie in bed and talk to Him about my day. Sometimes I'd even pretend my pillow was His lap as I lay there in the darkness believing that the Light of the World was ever by my side. As soon as I learned to read, I was reading the

Bible. I wanted to know everything there was to know about Jesus and see what He had to say as well.

In my teen years I began to see Him as my best friend: an epic best friend who had died to save my life, one who knew everything about me and loved me, and would never leave my side. My family went through some difficult seasons of extreme poverty, and I saw His hand in providing food and even a car, just when we needed those things the most.

In my early twenties I read a book, *Your Knight in Shining Armor* by P. "Bunny" Wilson, that talked about going on dates with Jesus, and I didn't have to think twice about incorporating that into my life. I'd plan picnics, walks, movies, and long drives all with the purpose of spending alone time with Jesus. Just before the first of these dates, one of my best friends had a couple of roses delivered to my house. Jesus seemed to coordinate the timing of their delivery: They showed up just as I was about to leave.

STRAINED RELATIONSHIP

As beautiful as my relationship with Jesus was, I knew His deep love wasn't just for me but for everyone. The more I learned about Him, the more I loved Him and wanted to be like Him—especially in how He loved others.

By the time I was 23, while all my friends were graduating from college, I felt that Jesus was finally calling me to *go* to college. I picked a Protestant Christian college where I planned to major in the Bible and theology, because I knew that however I served the Lord, those two subjects would be helpful. I also wanted to write books that would help people grow closer to Jesus, so I tacked on a major in journalism to sharpen my writing skills.

I saw this time as a huge adventure—setting out into the world to begin a life of learning more about Jesus and ministering to others in His name. The hardest part was leaving all my friends and especially my family behind, but I trusted that living life for Jesus was worth the sacrifice.

My first semester was amazing, but by finals week things with my family were falling apart. I'd grown up in a broken home full of divorce, poverty, and neglect, and as the oldest of my siblings I felt a great responsibility to take care of everyone. I was convinced that if I had stayed everything would have been fine, and I grew to feel a new emotion toward Jesus: anger. I began to blame Him for my family falling apart. After all, He was God, which meant He had known what would happen to my family if I left. And yet He had asked me to take a leap of faith and go to college.

Since I now found myself angry at the very person I was studying, I considered quitting school, but I felt like Jesus was asking me to stay. Despite my anger, I remained. I now found myself pretending to have affection for Jesus while harboring deep anger and resentment toward Him.

I lived with this inner conflict for a couple of years: studying the Bible, going to church, and serving in ministry, all while being unable to let go of my anger toward Jesus. I even began daydreaming about quitting school and starting a brand-new life that didn't involve Him or Christianity. I couldn't imagine letting go of my anger, and I figured quitting would be easier. Then I would no longer feel like a hypocrite and wouldn't have to think about my broken relationship with Him—the former love of my life.

Of course, Jesus knew what was in my mind and heart. I still talked to Him, but I avoided addressing my anger with Him, which made my relationship with Him extremely uncomfortable.

And then the unexpected happened. Jesus gave me permission to leave Him. I had been daydreaming, per usual, about leaving school and living my non-Christian, non-Jesus life when that still, small voice spoke into my heart.

"You are free to go."

It's easy to get lost in a daydream about the grass being greener on the other side of a fence that you think you'll never cross. But when given the opportunity to actually cross the fence, you'll find out whether or not the dream has substance. In being told I was free to go, my real feelings were immediately revealed.

My heart dropped to the pit of my stomach—not at the very real thought of leaving everything behind, but at the thought of living my life without Jesus.

My response to Jesus was immediate: "Where else would I go, Lord?! You alone have the words of eternal life! Wait . . . did I just quote Scripture?"

I burst out laughing. My heart was revealed. I wanted to complain, but I didn't actually want to go anywhere. This reality sunk in even more as I reflected on the passage of Scripture I had quoted. They were the words of Saint Peter in the Book of John, Chapter 6. Jesus had just talked about the importance of eating His flesh and blood only to have a bunch of His followers, understandably horrified and confused, leave Him.

> Jesus then said to the Twelve, "Do you also want to leave?" Simon Peter answered him, "Master, to whom shall we go? You have the words of eternal life. We have come to believe and are convinced that you are the Holy One of God." (John 6:67–69, NABRE)

In that moment, the bitterness I'd been holding on to for years faded away. In His deep love and compassion for me, Jesus had held up a mirror for me to see my heart. I knew that I didn't want a life without Christ, and that I needed to work through my feelings in order to heal my relationship with Him.

The next Sunday, I made Him a promise—one that I have made every Sunday since: "I love You, Jesus . . . and I will continue to follow You . . . no matter what." I had made it through a season of doubt, and found my faith in Jesus to be more sure, and our relationship to be stronger than ever.

JESUS AND THE CATHOLIC CHURCH

And then Jesus led me to the Catholic Church.

By my early thirties my impression of Catholicism was that it had little to do with Jesus, and given how important

He was to me, that meant I wanted nothing to do with Catholics.

The Catholic Church seemed to be all about the pope, Mary, the saints, priests, monks, nuns, rituals, rosaries, and extravagant churches. I saw pictures and statues of Jesus here and there, but they seemed to be obscured by everything else, like He was a forgotten mascot.

But when I set aside what I thought the Catholic Church was and started looking at the Church objectively (though still skeptically), I began to see Jesus everywhere and central to everything. I saw Jesus in the life of my friend who was becoming Catholic. I saw Jesus in the devout Catholics who talked about Him with affection. I saw Jesus in the lives of the saints who lived and died for Him. I saw Jesus in art, architecture, liturgy, mass, prayer, the sacraments—especially Communion.

I had been afraid that all these "extras" would distract me from my relationship with Jesus. What I never anticipated was that they would only deepen my understanding of Him and my relationship with Him.

Until I became Catholic, my relationship with Jesus felt like it was all on me. I had to make time for church, read and memorize the Bible, make sure I prayed, surround myself with friends who would encourage me in my faith, read good books about Jesus, and so on. All of these things were good and helped me in my faith—but they were all up to me. This might sound funny, but it was almost like I had a one-sided relationship with Jesus. Oh sure, He would reach out—like with the arrival of my roses for our first date, or providing food for my family when we were poor—but it still felt like I'd had to put in a lot of work for Him to do those things.

There's this scene in the movie *Hitch* that kept coming to mind as I noticed this shift in how I related to Jesus as I became a Catholic. The character Hitch, played by Will Smith, makes his living teaching awkward guys how to be more charming in order to "get the girl" they're interested in. His main client in the movie is Albert, a shy accountant played by Kevin James. The scene that kept playing in my mind was when Hitch was teaching Albert how to get ready for his first kiss. Hitch explained that you need to lean in for the kiss 90 percent of the way, and then hold and let the girl come forward that last 10 percent.

An odd analogy, I know, but it's exactly how I felt! My whole life, I'd felt like I'd been leaning in that 90 percent in my relationship with Jesus while hoping and praying that He would show up and make up that last 10 percent. Now, granted—He did. So many times! But in retrospect, it felt like my relationship with Jesus was a lot of work. I had never questioned it, though, since it was all I'd ever known.

Enter the Catholic Church. I came to learn that all those things I had perceived as distractions from my relationship with Jesus were actually gifts from Him to aid in our relationship!

His mother, Mary, was the first to believe that her son was the savior of the world, and not only did she put her faith in Him, but she sacrificed a lot to do so, which made her an inspiration for me to love Jesus more sacrificially.

The saints were friends whose love and faith in Christ inspired me to be more like them as they strived to be more like Him. Written prayers, like the one at the beginning of this chapter, put words to the cries of my heart and often taught me more about my faith as well. And then there were the religious and the priests—people whose love for Jesus led them to abandon everything to serve Him.

These were all amazing new aids to encourage me in my faith, but the two places I met Christ most intimately were in confession and in Holy Communion. After years of ministering to others, confession was where I was ministered to. I had always confessed my sins directly to God, but then had to rely on my own faith and self-talk when I'd doubt if I was actually forgiven. In confession I was given the gift of an ear and a voice ordained by God to act *in persona Christi:* to hear my list of sins and then let me know that God forgave and absolved them, speaking to me on Christ's behalf.

In persona Christi is a Latin phrase meaning "in the person of Christ." Catholics don't believe that the priest is an intermediary between God and mankind (a common assumption among non-Catholics), but that he stands in the place of Christ as an authorized representative. This happens in two specific instances: in confession and during Mass. It is a grave responsibility and has to be taken seriously by those who are ordained, because the eternal consequences of acting counter to Christ in these two contexts is condemnation to hell. Good and holy priests are aware of this and take those roles very seriously, and with great humility and reverence.

Holy Communion at Mass was the second place I intimately met Christ. Catholics have believed from the beginning of Christianity that the piece of bread the priest prays over (consecrates) and then distributes at Mass becomes the very body, blood, soul, and divinity of Christ Jesus. In the Communion services I participated in as a Protestant, whatever spiritual benefit I was supposed to receive from Communion had to do with how strongly I believed or focused. In Catholicism, we believe that Jesus literally gives himself to us in Holy Communion, and that He is present in that little piece of bread no matter how we feel or if we are distracted or battling doubts. Once I accepted this truth about Holy Communion, I was at the church anytime the doors were open.

I'd spent a lifetime following Christ, going 90 percent in our relationship, always hoping in faith that He'd go that last 10 percent. I found in the Catholic Church that He'd set up an entire system where I didn't have to do all the work in my relationship with Him—I just had to show up. A lifelong burden fell off my shoulders, one I hadn't realized I'd been carrying. He was going the 90 percent now and I was going the 10 percent. I just had to show up and be. He would minister to me through His mother, through His saints, through His priests, through His sacraments—through His church.

And just around the corner, after I became Catholic, Jesus was about to open my eyes to another level of intimacy with Him. One that it seemed He'd been hinting at my entire life.

MARRIED TO JESUS

On August 14, 2016, I was camping near Crater Lake in Southern Oregon with some friends when I woke up early one morning from a recurring nightmare. The dream was always the same: I was in a church, dressed in a wedding dress and ready to walk down the aisle. All my friends and family were there but the groom was nowhere to be seen. In fact, I never knew who I was about to marry! I'd anxiously stand there in my wedding dress filled with fear and doubt. Who was this guy? My friends and family seemed to approve, but I wasn't sure that I did. I'd be sick to my stomach as I walked down the aisle, dreading the vow I was about to make. The dream would always end before the groom ever got there.

I'd been having that same dream a couple times a year since my early twenties. When I woke that morning, I lay in bed and reflected on this nightmare that had plagued me for over ten years. It had been almost a year since I'd become Catholic, and I had been trying to figure out what Jesus wanted me to do with my life. I noticed that it was 4:30 A.M., so I decided to get up and go for a stroll to watch the sunrise.

I used to joke that I'd had a crush on every guy I'd ever met. Some crushes lasted a minute or two and others quite a bit longer, with the dream of marriage always on my mind. And yet, since becoming Catholic I couldn't stop thinking about becoming a sister. In the Catholic Church, sisters who make their vows are married to Jesus and will often even wear a wedding ring showing their commitment to Christ. I had learned that nuns were married to Jesus while I was in high school and loved the idea, but since I hadn't been Catholic I'd had to settle for my little dates with Jesus.

However, I was Catholic now. That shifted the idea of being married to Jesus into the realm of reality, and I couldn't shake the thought.

My stroll took me to a dock sitting on Diamond Lake, the sight of our campgrounds. I walked out and sat at the end of the dock as traces of light began to fill the summer sky. Why did I keep having this dream? I'd never had any issues with marriage, and yet this dream haunted me. I thought back over my life and mused about my many crushes. All of them had something in common: They all loved Jesus and, on some level, they all *reminded* me of Jesus. While that wasn't a surprise to me, I felt like I was seeing it in a brand-new way. Just as slowly as the sun shed light while rising, so Jesus began to shed light onto my heart's true desires. I saw in my desire for romance and marriage and love a deeper desire—for Him. I reflected on my relationship with Jesus through the years: His faithfulness, His protection, His guidance, His comfort, His love.

The thought struck me that I was like the leading lady in a romantic comedy. There was always some guy I was interested in, and all the while my guy-best-friend who was head-over-heels in love with me waited in the friend zone for the moment He could finally sweep in and be with me.

"Oh, Jesus." I laughed out loud, breaking the silence of

that cool morning. "Here I am, interested in every guy out there while You're the patient best friend who is actually in love with me."

My laughter faded fast as I realized the statement I'd just made wasn't a joke. I felt as though Jesus was suddenly very real and very present on that dock—very lovingly and seriously agreeing with what I'd just said.

"Oh my . . ." I whispered. "You really *are* the patient best friend who is in love with me."

I was quiet again. I knew at that moment Jesus was inviting me on another journey—He was calling me to seek Him further in religious life. I still had a lot to work through before I'd be ready to make any big decisions about being a sister or a nun, but I now knew this was the path He was asking me to take. I felt like I was being proposed to.

Soberly, I said yes.

On August 14, 2020—four years to the day that Jesus proposed to me on a dock on Diamond Lake, I officially entered religious life—freely following my patient best friend and the many adventures He had in store for me.

The wedding nightmares never returned.

CHAPTER 2

Is Catholicism Christianity?

For all thy Church, O Lord, we intercede; Make thou
our sad divisions soon to cease; Draw us the nearer
each, to each we plead, By drawing all to thee, O
Prince of Peace; Thus may we all one bread, one body
be, Through this blest Sacrament of Unity.

—W. H. TURTON, "Lord, Who at Thy First
Eucharist Didst Pray"

Having grown up Protestant, I was raised with the firm understanding that Catholics weren't Christians. I don't know where this idea first came from, but I rarely questioned it. I can recall a Catholic gal visiting a college Bible study I attended at my church. All of us treated her with the utmost kindness while not believing for one moment that she was a Christian. In fact, I can remember us debriefing the experience after she left, thinking how odd it was that a Catholic would want to come to a Bible study.

So imagine my surprise years later when I saw one of my new Catholic friends, CJ, wearing a T-shirt that said, CATHOLICISM. EST. 33 A.D. The year 33 is believed to be the year Jesus died and, according to Christians, also rose again. It's the year the disciples began to tell the world about Jesus. It's the year Christianity began, and when followers of Jesus became known as Christians.

A deep well of anger boiled up within me. How dare Catholics claim to have been established by Jesus way back at the beginning. They're the ones who messed everything up. Who do they think they are?

Not only had I been raised to think Catholics weren't Christians, but I had also been raised to believe that at some point after the apostles (Jesus's followers) died, Christianity lost its way and no longer followed the teachings of Christ. I'd been told it was the fault of "the Catholics," though the reasons changed: Catholics focused too much on Mary and the saints, they followed the pope instead of Jesus, they worshipped idols, they thought donating money could save their souls, they did good works to earn their salvation, they followed empty traditions—and the list went on and on.

Christianity was no longer what it was supposed to be, because of Catholics.

As it was explained to me, this problem wasn't fixed until the 1500s, with the Protestant Reformation. Nearly everything that happened before that period was a distortion of the true Christian faith that Christ had established, and the ones to blame for this distortion were the Catholics.

Did I have proof? No. Had I looked into it myself? No. But, my goodness, I would have died on that hill. So the arrogant claim on CJ's shirt was like a slap in the face and, from my perspective, a flat-out lie.

IGNORANCE IN ISOLATION

I was in my early teens the first time I realized there were other Christians in the world that weren't part of the Christian and Missionary Alliance (CMA) church I attended. The little CMA church I was raised in was the same church my great-grandpa Charlie helped build, and where my grandpa Phil had been pastor for a season; it was the church my mom grew up in, that my parents met and were married in; the church I'd attended for the first nine years of my life. Even when we moved to a new area an hour away, we found another CMA church to attend.

As the years went on, I met Christians from a variety of denominations: Baptists, Nazarenes, Evangelicals, Pentecostals, Charismatics, Methodists, Quakers, and even Christians whose churches weren't part of a denomination. Each group said they loved Jesus, but we all seemed to love Him differently and even believed different things about Him. While I got along with everyone from these different denominations just fine, the fact that we weren't all on the same page didn't sit well with me . . . but I didn't know why. After all, we all loved Jesus, right? Isn't that what a Christian is? Someone who loves and follows Jesus?

A few years later, I found myself reading John 17, in which Jesus prays right before his arrest and eventual crucifixion. In the first half of the chapter, Jesus prays for His disciples, but then the subject of His prayer shifts:

"I pray not only for them, but also for those who will believe in me through their word, so that they may all be one, as you, Father, are in me and I in you, that they also may be in us, that the world may believe that you sent me. And I have given them the glory you gave me, so that they may be one, as we are one, I in them and you in me, that they may be brought to perfection as one, that the world may know that you sent me, and that you loved them even as you loved me." (John 17:20–23, NABRE)

My little teenage brain nearly exploded. *Jesus . . . is praying . . . for me?* I mean, I believed in Him through His disciples' word—albeit many, many years removed. But still! Jesus *is* praying for me— *No, not just for me. For us!*

I read those verses over and over and over again. I couldn't believe such a passage in the Bible existed! Had I heard a sermon about it? Did everyone know about this passage? Why weren't we all talking about this all the time? Why weren't we doing something to solve the divisions between us? I was full of questions and hungry for answers.

Everyone I mentioned it to seemed to have the same response: "Oh, that's cool . . ."

I eventually calmed down. I wanted to understand why Jesus prayed for us to be one, and why we weren't one. From my perspective, no one seemed interested in doing anything about it. Given that I was only in high school, I decided to hold this passage in my heart as a constant prayer until I was older, wiser, more educated . . . and could perhaps do something to help this prayer come to fruition.

DISAGREEMENTS AND DIVISIONS

The Protestant Christian university I attended for college and eventually for my master's degree considered itself "interdenominational," which meant Christians from nearly all denominations were welcome (except Catholic and Orthodox Christians). The school was a melting pot of Christianity; the professors were from a variety of Christian backgrounds and, despite all their theological disagreements, seemed to agree on the main tenets of Christianity: the Bible being the inspired Word of God; Jesus being the eternal Son of God who became human, lived a perfect life, was crucified and rose again to save us from our sins; and that God exists as a Trinity (Father, Son, and Holy Spirit).

One of my college friends used to say, "In essentials unity, in non-essentials liberty, in all things charity," which is a quote attributed to a variety of possible Christian authors throughout the ages. It seemed like my school was the embodiment of Christian unity. I began to see these divisions between Christians as normative and almost necessary, given the many differences in cultures, backgrounds, and perspectives.

I even started celebrating these divisions.

When I learned that October 31, 1517, was the day that a German Catholic priest named Martin Luther submitted a list of issues he had with the Catholic Church, thereby sparking the Protestant Reformation, I joined my friends in annual "Reformation Day" celebrations. It felt like a nerdy Christian version of Independence Day.

And why not celebrate the Reformation? Martin Luther had been the main advocate of the principle of *sola scriptura,* which is the Latin for "Scripture alone." It is the idea that the Bible is the only authority for teaching the Christian faith, and that we have no need for the Catholic Church to interpret or explain Scripture to us. Some Christian groups even purport that nothing in Christianity should be done unless it is found either explicitly or implicitly in the Bible, which means all the dogmas and traditions of the Catholic Church are deemed unnecessary. After all, the Bible doesn't explicitly mention things like the Immaculate Conception of Mary or fasting during Lent. Some see *sola scriptura* as a basis for Christians to claim freedom from the supposed control and false teachings of the Catholic Church.

Years later, as I was researching the Catholic Church, I asked one of my professors about his thoughts on this subject. He wasn't Catholic, but had studied at a Catholic school for his doctoral degree so I figured he'd have some special insight. At that point I was hoping someone would give me a good reason to stop looking into Catholicism.

He had some good arguments against Catholicism, many of which I'd heard before in some of my classes. However, I noticed he kept stating that although he disagreed with certain things about Catholicism, other Protestants had no problems with them—though they took issue with other aspects of the faith.

A realization washed over me: Those of us who were non-Catholic Christians didn't only have a love of Jesus in common. We all seemed to also agree that the Catholic Church was wrong (though our reasons varied). I felt a pit in my stomach. I'd always thought that the version of Christianity I'd been raised in, schooled in, and went to church in was unified under a singular love of Jesus; but I now realized we were also unified in our disagreement with the Catholic Church.

MISSING YEARS AND MISSING FAMILY

In my exploration of the Catholic Church and its claims to be the church founded by Christ, I started learning about what the Church looked like up until the major fractures of the 1500s. Was it really as bad as I'd thought?

The answer was mixed. There were periods of corruption, indulgence in wealth, promulgation of false teachings, bad priests, bad bishops, and bad popes. But between these periods, and even intertwined with them, were seasons of correction and healing. The Church even took Martin Luther's criticisms seriously and made adjustments.

I found that there was profound good that was done. Followers of Jesus sacrificially served the poor and downtrodden, performed miracles, and shared the good news of God's love and sacrifice. I also found men and women who, like Luther, challenged the Church when she veered in the wrong direction, but who stayed in the faith and brought about change from within.

I found that when false teachings about Jesus or the Christian life would spring up, the Church would step in to clarify, correct, and dispel what was being promulgated so that the purity of the Gospel remained intact. I learned that when the Church issues dogmas, which are indisputable teachings, it is to solidify a truth about Jesus that is being debated.

What I'd always seen as a distortion of the teachings of Jesus and an overreach of the Catholic Church was actually a safeguard to ensure the truth about Jesus and His gift of salvation. In fact, I learned that the task of bishops is to ensure the preservation of the truth of the teachings of and about Jesus as handed down by the apostles themselves— a two-thousand-year-old safeguard. I began to see the Church as less of a control freak and more of a loving mother: a mother I'd been kept from my entire life.

I began to feel a growing sadness and resentment at being taught that the Catholic Church messed things up. I felt like I was meeting a family that I had been kept from. My annual celebration of the separation of Protestant Christians from the Catholic Church became a day of mourning. Jesus's prayer in John 17 came to my mind more and more as I realized how far from unity Christians actually were, and how the Catholic Church had been actively trying to heal our divisions and get us all back on track while maintaining the truth of the Gospel of Jesus. And I realized my friend CJ's shirt might actually be right after all, though actually accepting or admitting this was still a ways off.

GOING TO THE PERIPHERY

Around this time, I began attending a Catholic prayer group with a group of young Catholic adults. I had traded places with that Catholic girl who'd visited my church's Bible study all those years ago, and I fully expected to be looked at like some sort of spectacle as well. Quite the opposite was true. They were genuinely excited to meet me! They invited me to dinner after we finished praying, and even listened intently as I shared my thoughts on Lent during a post-dinner discussion on the topic of fasting. I had been shocked by the beautiful experience of praying vespers and compline with them, and even more surprised by the way they welcomed me with open arms.

When I decided to go back the following week, I was greeted with the same genuine smiles. Everyone made me feel like I was a part of the group, even though I was the only Protestant in the room. After prayer that evening, we got together for dinner at one of their homes. Just like the previous week, our dinner conversations transitioned into a post-dinner discussion. This time the topic was about the "peripheries" in each of our lives—those people who we wouldn't normally interact or associate with. I didn't have any thoughts on the subject, so I decided to listen.

At one point, Father Luan, one of the two priests who prayed vespers with the group, entered the conversation by saying that he'd been thinking about me since the last time we'd all been together. All eyes turned to me. *Here it comes.*

It's time to talk about the elephant in the room. He's going to call me out for being Protestant. I knew everything was going too well . . .

Imposter syndrome began to settle in as I waited to hear about the "non-believer" in their midst. Instead, Father Luan told everyone that he'd been thinking about me since last week, because I inspired him. *A Catholic priest is inspired . . . by me?* Father explained that for people to step outside their comfort zone and get to know others takes a lot of courage. And here I was, a Protestant stepping outside of my comfort zone to come spend time with a bunch of Catholics. He reiterated how touched and inspired he'd been by that, and even more so when I decided to come back and spend more time with them.

I went home that evening thinking about Jesus's prayer for unity in John 17. This was the first time I'd seen that prayer lived out. The Catholics I was spending time with were confident in their faith, but that didn't stop them from listening to me talk about mine. And their interest in me helped me feel comfortable asking questions about their faith. They didn't see me as anything other than a Christian who loved Jesus, and I was beginning to learn how to see them the same way.

ONE QUESTION

I was surprised, inspired, challenged, and encouraged in my faith as I got to know the other side of Christian history and family that I'd felt kept from. I also experienced a sort of spiritual vertigo. I began questioning everything. Was CJ's shirt actually true, and if so, what did that mean for me?

I felt frozen in place. I was terrified of the idea of becoming Catholic, but I also felt that the faith I was raised with was lacking, though I couldn't figure out why.

I decided to schedule a meeting with the priest at the Catholic Church I'd been visiting. Father Boyle was a tall, thin man with a proper English accent. He'd recently been assigned as pastor of the parish I'd been visiting and seemed like someone that might have some answers.

I poured my heart out to him: bits of my life story in addition to the details of this new ecclesial crisis of faith. He sat patiently and listened the whole time. At the end I admitted that I saw Truth in the Catholic Church, even if there were still things I disagreed with or didn't understand; and because of that, I didn't know what to do.

After a few silent, reflective moments he replied to my essay-long monologue with elegant simplicity.

"Well, there's really only one question you need to ask yourself," he said. "Is the Catholic Church the church that Jesus Christ founded?"

I was dumbfounded. All of my wrestling and research, questions and doubts, truly were encapsulated in that concise question. If my answer was no, then I could go on with my life giving no more thought to the Catholic Church. This would have been merely a season where I learned something new and then moved on with my life.

But if the answer was yes . . .

If the answer was yes, then my doubts and fears, disagreements and questions, would be answered. Because if the Catholic Church was indeed the church that Jesus Christ founded on this earth to be the safeguard of the truth and to tell the world about Him; if the Catholic Church hadn't fallen away from or distorted Christianity but in fact had been refining doctrines, solidifying teachings, and continuing His work; if the Catholic Church was the Bride of Christ . . . then all I wanted was to end this five-hundred-year-long protest I was born into and return to my long-lost family.

Father Boyle broke my silent contemplation. "Do you know how to answer that question?"

I felt all the blood drain from my face as I looked up at him and nodded my head.

"Yes," I said slowly and cautiously. I was afraid of my answer and what it meant. Up until that point I had only been researching the Catholic Church to understand it better. However, it seemed I had veered off that initial path and was now on a very personal journey of faith and truth.

My voice was shaky as I answered his initial question. "Yes, I think the Catholic Church is the church that Jesus established."

ROME SWEET HOME

Less than one year after I was received into the Catholic Church, I went on a pilgrimage to Italy with Father Boyle, some of my new Catholic friends, and a handful of other folks from around the United States. We visited Norcia, Assisi, a variety of holy sites in southern Italy, and of course, Rome and the Vatican.

During my time in Rome we visited a variety of churches, saw amazing art, historical sites, and beautiful scenery; but what stuck with me were the tombs of the early Christians. After spending all that time researching the "missing years" of my faith, I now found myself in front of the graves of Christians who had lived and died trying to preserve the truth of the faith I now held. After all, for the first three hundred years of the Church, Christianity was illegal, which meant becoming a Christian was to accept the possibility of a gruesome death sentence.

As a Protestant Christian, I'd always wondered what had happened to the bodies of those early Christians. In Rome I found them lovingly cared for, and even displayed for the multitudes of pilgrims who come to pay their respects.

My feelings of gratitude increased as we visited the Basilica of Saint Paul Outside the Walls and saw the grave of Saint Paul himself—originally one of the biggest opponents–turned–biggest promulgators of Christianity. I'd read his words my entire life, since he'd written much of the New Testament—and now here I was, right in front of his earthly remains.

And then we went to the Vatican. We were there to celebrate a High Latin Mass at the altar of the chair of Saint Peter, which is in the back of Saint Peter's Basilica under the beautiful stained-glass window of the Holy

Spirit in the form of a dove. When Mass was over, security quickly set out to move us along so they could block off the area. My friends and I were making our way through the crowd when we saw Father Boyle, who had separated from us in order to celebrate the Mass with the other priests there.

Father Boyle quickly pointed in the direction of the area near the tomb of Saint Peter, the first pope. He directed us to seize the opportunity and pray the Apostles' Creed in front of the tomb while we had the chance.

The Apostles' Creed, a basic statement of the truths of the Christian faith, was developed in the earliest centuries of the Church. Each line in the creed proclaims what is central to the faith of Christians. It's also the first prayer said when praying the Rosary, so I had it memorized by then.

We hurried over to where Father Boyle had instructed and dropped to our knees. In unison we began praying:

"I believe in God, the Father almighty,
Creator of heaven and earth;
and in Jesus Christ, His only Son our Lord,
who was conceived by the Holy Spirit,
born of the Virgin Mary,
suffered under Pontius Pilate,
was crucified, died and was buried;
He descended into hell;
on the third day He rose again from the dead;
He ascended into Heaven,

and is seated at the right hand of God the Father al-
mighty;
from there He will come to judge the living and the dead.
I believe in the Holy Spirit, the holy catholic Church,
the communion of saints, the forgiveness of sins,
the resurrection of the body, and life everlasting. Amen."

As we prayed, I was overwhelmed with the realization that Saint Peter, who was buried below me, had died for preaching the truths of this creed. Tears of gratitude rolled down my cheeks as I realized that I was back home in the Church that had spent thousands of years living and dying to preserve the faith and truth of Jesus Christ. A faith I'd always held—even while separated from it.

ROLES REVERSED

I was working at my alma mater, that very Protestant university I mentioned earlier, when I was received into the Catholic Church, and I wondered how they would feel about one of their alumni/employees converting. Anxiously, I let my boss know of my plans and was surprised when she said I'd be able to continue working there. I just had to sign the school's doctrinal statement, a document outlining their beliefs about Christianity, and I wasn't allowed to try converting any of the students.

I was relieved at her response. I really didn't want to have to find another job, especially since I loved the one I had, but I also knew that the school's doctrinal statement was basic enough that it didn't go against the Catholic faith. And I've never been good at evangelizing others, so I certainly wasn't worried about that at all. In fact, I'd go so far as to say that I was awful at it. I once had a student ask me how to pray the Rosary and I awkwardly laughed at her instead of offering to help. That said, word got around among the student body that there was a Catholic on staff, and every semester I'd get a student here and there wandering down the hall to ask me a question about the Catholic Church.

One such afternoon, an older student with a friendly smile dropped by to talk. He told me he'd heard I was Catholic, and wondered if that was true. I said it was. He sat back and seemed reflective. He seemed to be searching for the right words for what I thought might be another question.

"It's okay. I'm not easily offended, so don't worry about how to say what you want to say," I assured him.

"Okay." He sighed. "Well, I don't believe you're a Christian at all. Catholics can't be Christians."

I couldn't help but laugh at his blunt honesty. I'd come full circle and was faced with a version of who I used to be, sitting right across from me. After years of wrestling with my own questions, doubts, and presumptions, I felt very comfortable in such a seemingly uncomfortable conversation. I couldn't help but think of all the people I'd said the same thing to, and the patience they had with me when my questions were just as blunt.

I may not have figured out how to heal the divisions in Christianity, but since becoming Catholic I've focused on at least clearing up five hundred–plus years of misunderstandings and misinformation with those curious enough to ask. Sometimes those I talk to decide to become Catholic themselves, and other times they at least gain a better understanding of Christianity, Catholicism, and their own faith. If Christians are to be known for their love of God and neighbor, being willing to have hard conversations and learn from each other is at least a small step in that direction. And, hopefully, a step toward the unity that Jesus himself prayed for.

CHAPTER 3

What Is Sin and Salvation, and What Are the Sacraments?

GRANDMA CAROL

The first Catholic I knew was my stepdad's mom, Grandma Carol, a German nurse who loved her cigarettes, vodka, and cussing. One Christmas, as we were gathering around the dining room table, folks were chatting and someone used the Lord's name in vain, saying "Jesus Christ" as an expletive. Grandma Carol snapped from the kitchen, "*Hey!* Don't talk like that on the Lord's Day!"

I was surprised at her chastisement, because not only did most of her kids use Jesus's name as an expletive, but she often did too! So her rebuke on this special occasion struck me as hypocritical. After all, if using foul language is so bad, why avoid it only on special occasions?

Growing up Protestant, I was taught that people who loved Jesus and were "saved" didn't smoke, drink, or cuss.

So, in my twelve-year-old eyes, this Catholic woman, with all her vices, was blindly stumbling toward hell. She may have gone to daily mass, prayed her Rosary, and gone to confession, but I believed those were just empty actions that didn't have any impact on her spiritual growth and—obviously, from my perspective—didn't help her give up her sins. I imagined all Catholics to be like Grandma Carol: going through the motions of an ancient religion while stuck in their sinful lives. They might confess their sins to a priest, but it didn't seem to be doing them any good.

At least, that's what I thought.

My understanding of sin and salvation was shortsighted. I was overly focused on actions, not the thoughts and movements of the heart that precipitate those actions, or the forgiveness always ready to embrace a repentant repeat-offending rule-breaker. And I wasn't ready to see myself as that repeat offender in need of grace.

SIN, FREE WILL, AND "THE RULES"

The Catechism of the Catholic Church, a large document that explains the teachings of Christianity, states that "Sin is an offense against reason, truth, and right conscience; it is failure in genuine love for God and neighbor caused by a perverse attachment to certain goods. It wounds the nature of man and injures human solidarity."[*]

---

[*] Catechism 1849

When God created humanity, He did so in order to have a relationship with us, and sin is what breaks that relationship. This is a theme woven throughout Scripture and is understood by all Christians. God is the embodiment of life and love, and He brought both to His Creation. God didn't force people to love and obey Him, though: He allowed them the ability to exercise free will and decide for themselves. According to the Book of Genesis, the first humans broke their perfect relationship with God by rejecting the life He gave them and trying to be like Him instead. This resulted in sin entering the world, and with it all the pain and consequences of a life apart from God.

Separation from God means losing eternal life and perfect love, because God *is* life and perfect love. Human life was frustrated by death, and human love became intermingled with selfishness and pride. People became caught in the predicament we all know so well: having both the desire to do good and the temptation to do evil.

That temptation is what can make things so difficult and confusing. From a young age, we sense that certain things are wrong. Even as kids we'd get that pit in our stomach or a guilty feeling when we knew we'd done something wrong. I can recall bringing home a box of candy bars to sell for a school fundraiser when I was in preschool. I don't recall being told not to eat them, but I knew they had a purpose and that I shouldn't. That wasn't enough to stop me from hiding under the kitchen table and devouring one before being caught. I didn't need to be told I was doing something wrong—I knew full well.

But sometimes the line between what is permissible and what is sinful can get fuzzy and it would be helpful to have some guidelines. Thankfully, God gave us some basic rules to help us understand the difference between good and evil: the Ten Commandments. In these rules, you can see that sin is not only a matter of breaking one's relationship with God, but also damaging relationships with others. The first four Commandments describe how to love God, while the last six describe how to love others.

So now that humanity knew the rules, they followed them perfectly, right? Well, not really. People seemed to focus on finding loopholes.

As a teacher, I can empathize. Part of my ministry as a religious sister is to teach first-grade students at the local Catholic school. Our class rules exist to help my kids learn, grow, and have a good relationship with each other and with me. They know this—and they even want it! Especially when it means a class party or earning a special prize. But do all these benefits help them make wise choices? Nope. I wish they would! I actually had one student whose good behavior had earned her a prize from the prize box, but while she was picking out her prize I caught her trying to steal a second one! As much as we want all the benefits that come from avoiding sin and doing good . . . we still choose evil. We begin to question the rules and come up with ways to justify our desires.

Each of us can look through the Ten Commandments and find at least one we struggle with, and most of us can count several. Even sins done in secret impact our relationship with God and our relationships with others. What we often forget, though, is that all of these sins hurt us as well. God's rules aren't just to tell us what to avoid so that we don't upset Him or someone else. He knows the impact they have on our own lives.

Again, I see this in my students. I often feel bad for the ones who get in trouble the most, because I see how frustrated they are with themselves when they have to suffer the consequences of yet another bad choice. What they don't often see is that the consequences I give them are meant to help them make a better choice in the future.

But rules, laws, and commandments were never going to bring us back into a perfect relationship with God. In fact, they weren't meant to. They were there to act as signs to show us how far from God we are.

I don't know about you, but I've seen plenty more sins than appear to be covered by that simple list. For example, what about the sin of gossip? If you've ever had someone gossip about you, then you know the damage it does.

The Ten Commandments are an umbrella under which all other sins are sorted. So gossip, which has the power to destroy a person's reputation and possibly even their life, is understood as a violation of the Sixth Commandment—*You shall not kill*. You may not have physically killed the person you gossiped about, but by slandering them with lies or even sharing something that's true but shouldn't have been shared, you are murdering their reputation—how they are viewed by others—and that may have a destructive effect on their lives.

VENIAL VS. MORTAL SINS

In most of the churches I attended before becoming a Catholic, people were taught that once you gave your life to Christ, you were saved for life. It didn't matter how sinful you were or what sins you continued to struggle with. Nothing you could ever do would change that.

But most people, myself included, believed that only to a point. The minute we heard about a Christian who had a drug problem, or who had sex outside of marriage, we immediately questioned whether they were actually saved. We would always say that all sins were equally wrong, but we also harbored an unspoken sense that they actually varied in severity. Even with friends and family who I knew had a vibrant faith, if they fell into one of those "big" sins, I began to doubt if they'd actually been saved to begin with. I experienced this firsthand when I became Catholic. A lot of my friends and family questioned whether I was still saved. Apparently, becoming Catholic counted as one of those big sins as well.

Being a Christian then became a game of steering clear of those "big-ticket" sins that would call into question my salvation, all while hiding the deeper internal sins that were able to roam free in my heart.

The funny thing about seeing a difference between big-ticket sins and little hidden sins is that even though it went against what I'd been taught in the Protestant churches I'd always attended, it wasn't far from what the Catholic Church teaches.

The Catholic Church breaks sin up into two categories: venial sins and mortal sins. Venial sins are the sins we all commit that aren't severe in nature, but still damage our relationships with God and others. Lying is one of the most common of these, but using foul language, eating too much, minor gossip, and losing your temper would also be considered venial sins.

Mortal sins are those sins that are clearly severe in nature and yet we chose to do them anyway. Sins like murder, stealing, or cheating on a spouse do reprehensible damage to ourselves and our relationships with others, and they cut us off from our relationship with God. In fact, if one were to die in a state of mortal sin, they would be condemned to hell.

Learning this distinction sobered me up real fast and caused me to pay closer attention to the temptations I was giving in to. I mean, I didn't want to go to hell! Yet I also suddenly felt relieved, because I knew where the line was and could focus on not crossing it. I became less worried about what other people thought about me, and more about my relationship with God. My salvation was no longer dependent on the opinions and judgments of others, but on objective truth and my own actions.

I also realized that those sins I'd judged Grandma Carol for weren't mortal sins leading her on a fast track to hell. They were merely symptoms of her sinful humanity that she'd have to work through and probably repent of continually in confession . . . same as me. And I also understood now that both of us were always a decision away from not just venial sins, but mortal sins as well. I was no longer judging others for the sins I saw, but praying that they, along with myself, would avoid temptation to both venial and mortal sins.

FORGIVENESS AND SALVATION

When you face your own propensity to sin and begin to understand how much you hurt yourself, others, and God by the poor choices you make in life, the feelings of guilt and shame can be so overwhelming that you can feel hopeless. It's like a life-altering medical diagnosis: Everything stops, and you have to face what feels like an impossible problem.

I've been there.

After avoiding those big external sins my entire life, the internal sins that people didn't often see began to take over. I found myself making bad choices and hurting those around me. The weight of my guilt was almost too much to bear.

Around this time, I found myself sitting in a Catholic church. I was waiting for one of my Catholic friends, and instead of sitting in the car I decided to sit in a pew. The church was silent and empty. I felt small in comparison to its majestic stained-glass windows, vaulted ceiling, and huge lifelike statues. My friend had told me that Catholic architecture and art was intended to communicate truths about God, humanity, and our need for salvation. The beauty and grandeur of that church reminded me of how big God was, and how little, insignificant, and broken I was. I noticed a crucifix hanging in the expanse between myself and the heights of the ceiling, and for the first time in my life felt my deep and desperate need for salvation and forgiveness.

Owning up to the things we've done wrong, and facing the pain we've caused others, can be humbling at best and crippling at worst. Life can begin to seem impossibly hopeless and painful. Even if we receive forgiveness from those around us, the weight of guilt lingers. It's like being told you have cancer but never finding out if there's a treatment.

But with sin there is not only a treatment; there's even a cure.

Jesus didn't come to earth just to be a good teacher or show us how to follow the rules, but to fix the mistake made by Adam and Eve and to restore humanity's relationship with God. This was done by His death on the cross and, most importantly, His resurrection and the life and love He brings to us through the sacraments.

SALVATION, BAPTISM, AND THE SACRAMENTS

I had been told as a little girl that in order to be saved from my sins, all I had to do was pray a simple prayer asking Jesus to forgive me and come into my life—and so I did! Years later, when I was in high school, I was in a small group that taught us how to lead someone to salvation. I was given a list of verses that all described salvation as coming from Christ—but none of them said anything about praying the little prayer I had for so long been encouraged to pray, or about leading others in that prayer. I figured that for such a crucial act there must be a passage that prescribes it. When I raised my hand and asked for such a passage, I was met with confused and blank stares. I wasn't questioning the importance of praying that prayer, but I was curious about why I hadn't heard a verse that explicitly stated that's what we were supposed to do.

The passage in the Bible that came closest to answering my question was in the Book of Acts. Paul and Silas, two men who had become Christians shortly after Jesus rose from the dead, were sitting in prison after being arrested for casting a demon out of a slave girl. When her owners realized they could no longer make a profit off her, they dragged Paul and Silas before the rulers of the city, made false accusations, and had them thrown in prison.

However, that night there was a huge earthquake during which all the doors flew open and everyone's chains were loosened—bad news for the jailer in charge! In fact, when he woke up and realized what had happened, he was about to kill himself out of fear for the punishment he figured was to come for all these prisoners getting out on his watch. But he was stopped by one of those prisoners! Saint Paul called out and let him know they were all still there.

The jailer's response to this miracle was to ask what he needed to do to be saved. Saint Paul said, "Believe in the

Lord Jesus and you and your household will be saved" (Acts 16:31, NABRE). The jailer, as well as his family, were all baptized immediately.

This jailer asked how to be saved and was told to believe in Jesus. And his belief was immediately followed by baptism. This was something I'd overlooked, because I'd always been told that baptism was symbolic; that it didn't do anything other than outwardly show a spiritual conversion that had already taken place in someone's heart. However, the Catholic Church teaches that there is a greater significance to baptism than I'd been raised to believe.

Catholics believe that baptism is the first treatment for our sinful condition, cleansing us from the inherited sin of our first parents. We enter the waters full of sin, and we leave the water sinless. The spiritual cancer has been removed from our system and we are in complete remission.

In the Book of Acts, Paul and Silas share the Gospel with a jailer who was charged with guarding them after they'd been arrested. After he believes their message, he and his family are baptized. This confused me, because I thought you had to intellectually understand and agree to salvation through Jesus in order to be baptized. This passage showed baptism to be more of a free gift for all—similar to the free gift of salvation—because that's what it is.

Baptism is our gateway into the spiritual life. Baptism cleanses us from sin and restores our relationship with God so that we are adopted as His children. It makes us receptive to the Holy Spirit helping us to avoid sin, and it begins our initiation into the Catholic Church.

Yes, you read that last part right. When I officially became Catholic, I didn't have to be re-baptized, because the Catholic Church considers any Trinitarian formula* of baptism as acceptable. A priest may do a "conditional" baptism if the details of the original are iffy, but the Church considers everyone out there who is baptized to be part of the Catholic Church.

Baptism is just the first of seven sacraments. A sacrament is a sure way we can meet Jesus through the ministry of the Catholic Church. Sacraments exist to help us grow in faith and holiness, and are the medicine of God's grace that Christ gives us. The sacraments of baptism, Holy Communion, and confirmation are known as the sacraments of initiation, because they bring you into the Church and prepare you to receive the other sacraments. Confession comes next, and is one of the two sacraments—the other being Holy Communion—that you can receive on a regular basis.

HOLY COMMUNION

This is my favorite sacrament—if one is permitted a favorite. The importance and efficaciousness of this sacrament is all about Jesus because, according to Catholic theology,

---

* The Trinitarian formula in baptism is "the name of the Father, the Son, and the Holy Spirit." Though just saying that you are baptized in this name isn't technically enough—those baptizing you (and you yourself if old enough) would need to agree with the Church's faith.

that "piece of bread" each person receives during Communion is the body, blood, soul, and divinity of Jesus Christ. As long as you are a Catholic who is free of mortal sin and go to confession at least once a year, you can receive Communion every single day—and even up to two times a day!

If we are all sick with sin, the Eucharist is our medicine. Christ, who is sinless, comes to us in the most humble form of bread; and the more we consume this heavenly medicine, the more like Christ we become. There are stories of saints who survived on nothing but the Eucharist, and I've even known people who suffer from celiac disease (a severe gluten allergy), and are deathly ill if they're exposed to flour, receive the Eucharist without harm.

One of the most important figures in the Church's history, Saint Augustine, who was a bishop in the North African city of Hippo, put it this way in his famous book *Confessions,* imagining that Jesus was addressing him directly: "I am the food of the fully grown; grow and you will feed on me. And you will not change me into you like the food your flesh eats, but you will be changed into me."* Catholics believe that when we receive the Eucharist, we truly receive Christ and are made members of his body.

We'll talk more about the Eucharist in the next chapter, so hang in there if you're stuck on a piece of bread becoming Jesus. I understand, I've been there . . . More to come!

---

* *Confessions,* Book VII, Chapter X (Oxford World's Classics translation)

CONFIRMATION

If baptism adopts us into the family of God, confirmation enlists us in the battle that is the Christian life. Through confirmation we are given an outpouring of the Holy Spirit, who gives us the strength and assistance needed to walk in a life of holiness.

I'd had a problem with baptism being for everyone—even babies—until I learned about confirmation. In the Catholic Church, children can receive the sacrament of confirmation once they've reached the age of eight, also known as the age of reason: They're old enough to understand what is happening and what they're getting themselves into.

Receiving the sacrament of confirmation is taking the faith you've been given as a child and making it your own. This is no longer just the faith you've been raised in, but one you chose to be in. That's why you choose a new name—one of a saint who will be your patron in the faith. (While the tradition of formally taking the name of your patron saint isn't practiced as much these days, choosing a patron saint still is.)

As we get older, the struggle with sin only seems to get more intense. With confirmation you receive an outpouring of the Holy Spirit (the third person of the Trinity), who can give you the strength to resist temptation and turn instead toward what is good, holy, and will help you grow in your faith and relationship with Christ.

Just a few years after I'd been received into the Church, I was asked to be a sponsor for a girl who was about to be confirmed. A sponsor is someone who not only attests to the spiritual readiness of the one wanting to be confirmed (the confirmand), but also commits to helping their confirmand continue to grow in their faith. Being asked to be a sponsor is both an honor and an important responsibility.

I asked this young woman how I could pray for her as she prepared for confirmation. After a moment of reflection, she asked me to pray that she be open to as much of the Holy Spirit as the Lord would like to give her. I was taken aback by the maturity and wisdom of her request. This girl understood what confirmation was all about and was ready to take the next step in her journey of faith.

CONFESSION

Notice that I mentioned baptism is our gateway into the spiritual life. While baptism does cleanse one from sin and restore that original relationship with God, what happens *after* baptism? Because we still sin: We snap at our kids; cheat on our time cards at work; indulge in too much food, drink, and spending; and lie to a cop to get out of a ticket. We don't need to be baptized again, but we need a remedy for the sins we continue to commit.

That's where confession comes in.

Thanks to Hollywood, I felt like I knew how to go to confession years before I ever became Catholic: You go into the confessional and a little window slides open showing a thin, see-through screen with a priest on the other side. You start with "Bless me, Father, for I have sinned. It's been X number of years since my last confession." Then a kind old priest with a thick Irish accent says something like "Oh, bless you, my child . . ." and then you tell him everything you've done wrong. For the most part, Hollywood made confession seem easy. Well, unless you had some really gnarly sins to confess.

When I started learning about the Catholic Church, I can't say I had any issues with the idea of confession—again, mostly thanks to Hollywood. That said, what I did have a *huge* problem with was some guy behind a screen in a box telling me my sins were forgiven. From my perspective, that was God's job, and the priest was an unnecessary middleman.

I started to think differently about confession while working as a resident director of a girls' dormitory at a Christian university. As the year progressed, some of the women would request to meet with me. Sometimes they just wanted a safe person to talk to about their crush, other times they wanted advice on their major, or their direction in life. But some were looking to be unburdened by sins they were carrying around in the depths of their souls.

I was never opposed to being someone safe they could share their heart with, but I realized I had no consolation to offer them other than to remind them of the same things they'd already been trying to remind themselves of: Jesus died for their sins, everything has already been forgiven, just keep trying to do better.

Confession wasn't an idea that was developed over the years, but was something Christ himself instituted as a ministry of forgiveness. He told his disciples, the founders of the Catholic Church, that they had the power to forgive sins. Now, that doesn't mean they are the initiators of forgiveness, but rather the dispensers of God's grace and forgiveness. The priest isn't a pointless middleman; he acts as the voice of Christ to absolve us of our sins and tell us we are forgiven.

The first time I went to confession, I felt sick over the idea of telling someone every sin I'd ever committed. I actually thought it seemed pointless, since I'd spent years already telling God about everything I'd ever done. Why did I need to tell some guy about it?

What I didn't expect was the feeling of freedom that came after that first confession. For the first time in my life, I actually felt unburdened. The old sins that used to come back and haunt me were laid to rest. I walked out of the confessional feeling truly free and full of the undeserved grace and forgiveness of God.

THE VOCATIONAL SACRAMENTS

While the first four sacraments are for every Catholic, the last three depend on the individual's situation in life. The sacrament of holy orders is bestowed upon men who are being ordained as deacons, priests, and bishops. The sacrament of marriage is enacted by couples married in the Catholic Church. The final sacrament is the anointing of the sick, and is for those in danger of death. This sacrament is especially sought out by those on their deathbed, because it cleanses people from sin if they are no longer able to confess their sins.

The sacraments of holy orders and marriage both focus on the vocations of the individuals receiving them. The term "vocation," which means *call,* is used in the Catholic Church to talk about the ministerial role the Lord is leading you to. Most people are called to married life, where their ministry is to help their spouse and, God willing, children to grow in holiness. Similarly, some men are called to the priesthood, where their ministry is also to help their spouse—the flock of believers entrusted to their care—to grow in holiness. The Holy Spirit is called into each vocation to equip those involved for their particular ministry and calling.

About a year before entering the Church, I was introduced to a guy who was a seminarian at the time and is now a priest. My vespers friends spoke highly of this Navy veteran, and I was curious about what had led him to pursue the priesthood. His answer not only stuck with me but impacted my own calling.

He told me that the reason he had pursued the priesthood wasn't that he couldn't find love with a woman. In fact, there *was* a woman he had loved, and likely always would. However, he didn't feel called to love only one person, but rather to love everyone. This future priest understood that at its core, the priesthood is about love. A love that is beyond sexual—and is purely sacrificial.

I was able to make it to his ordination as a deacon (the

step just before becoming a priest), and cried as I watched him lie facedown on the floor of the sanctuary of the church and pledge himself to God and in service to His people. This was the first ordination of any kind I had been to, and, although I'd participated in thirteen weddings myself and seen a lot of beautiful ceremonies, they all paled in comparison to the beauty of that moment.

A HAPPY DEATH

The thought of death had always scared me, and when I became a Catholic I was confused as to why people would talk about a "happy death." Even though I looked forward to seeing Jesus and being in heaven, I had never thought of death as a happy thing.

To a Catholic, a happy death is one where you are surrounded by family and friends, and are able, most importantly, to receive the anointing of the sick—known commonly as the "last rites." This sacrament acts as the beautiful final chapter of a full life. Ideally, an individual is baptized when they're born; receives all the sacraments at the proper ages, growing in holiness along the way; and then receives the gift of their final sacrament, the anointing of the sick, which, similar to baptism, cleanses them from sin.

The reason this is considered a happy death is because, in being cleansed from sin, you are more prepared to enter into heaven instead of going to purgatory.

I used to think purgatory was akin to hell, so much so that when debating its existence with a Catholic friend I burst into tears over the thought of going anywhere other than straight to heaven after I died. He helped me to understand that hell is for people who reject God and are therefore given what they want—to be separated from Him. Purgatory, however, is only for people who are going to heaven. Purgatory is a place to get rid of whatever attachments to sin we still maintain when we die, and you're only there as long as you need to be before joining Christ in heaven. I understood, but that didn't mean I liked it.

Per usual, I had a long chat with Jesus about it later that day. The tears came back as I ranted about how dumb a place like purgatory was. After all, it's not like I was very sinful. (This was back before I'd really started to understand my own sinfulness.) So why did I have to go to a place like that first? I wanted to see Jesus right away!

"If you're going to see Me either way, does it really matter how long it takes?" was the response I heard. I mumbled back, "No . . . not really," and then breathed a big sigh. Jesus had spoken up again, bringing calm to my chaos and reason to my emotions. His peace was welcome, even if a little begrudgingly since I still wanted to stew in my tantrum. He was right, though. And I appreciated His answer even more when I started to see how much sin I was (and am) still attached to, and how much growing in holiness was ahead of me.

And that is when I started to understand the beauty and gift of this final sacrament. I have no idea how much sin I'll have let go of by the time I die, but if there's anything I'm still stubbornly holding on to, I pray for a happy death—not only to be surrounded by loved ones, but, most importantly, to receive that final anointing so that I can cut my time in purgatory as short as possible. After all, I have a heavenly date with my beloved best friend: the savior of my soul.

"SAINT" PATRICK

One of the first Catholics I met on my journey to becoming a Catholic was a guy about my age named Patrick. Patrick reminded me of my Grandma Carol. He smoked, drank, and would unashamedly drop four-letter words here and there. Patrick was the first to admit that he was sinful. He didn't drink to excess, but he was aware that his smoking was unhealthy. He knew to hold his tongue in certain contexts, but he was glad to be able to speak freely when given the chance.

What I was too young to understand in my encounters with Grandma Carol, I was able to work out in my friendship with Patrick. He, just like Grandma Carol and the rest of us, struggled with sin. I'd spent my life trying to hide my sins for fear of the social ramifications they would have, while ignoring the sins that were eating away at my soul and my relationship with God. What I saw in Patrick was the acknowledgment and acceptance of his own sinful humanity, and the struggle all of us have to overcome our vices. I knew Patrick went to confession and that he was working on things with Jesus. I no longer questioned his or anyone else's salvation just because I could see their sin. After all, I had no idea what graces were being worked on behind the scenes and in the depths of their hearts. I could only focus on my own journey, and trust theirs to God.

CHAPTER 4

What Is the Mass and the Eucharist?

MY FIRST MASS

Despite my reservations about Catholicism, the first time I went to mass I was blindly optimistic. I was in college, and we'd been learning about the history of Christianity and the differences in Christian doctrines. My professor kept trying to get us to understand that Catholics were Christians—something the whole class seemed to initially disagree with him on.

One of our assignments that semester was to attend a couple of church services in denominations we knew little or nothing about. A Catholic mass was at the top of my list. Since my professor was so convinced they were Christians, I was curious to see for myself how they worshipped. My friends and I found a local parish that had mass on a Saturday night, which meant we could still go to our Protestant church services on Sunday morning. A winning option!

We walked into Saint Rita Catholic Church and took a seat toward the middle, with enough people in front of us that we could mimic their movements in order to blend in. The church was large and spacious with lots of windows, though these did little to bring any light in on that rainy Portland evening. I had been in some of the most beautiful Catholic churches in Paris when I was younger, and this one was drab by comparison with all the art, walls, windows, and pews varying in their respective degrees of brown, beige, and tan.

Mass started and I was immediately lost. Everything was in English but that didn't help. In contrast to my Protestant church, which was full of emotive worship songs and charismatic preaching, this mass seemed . . . boring. They did a couple readings from Scripture, which brought out my skeptical side, since I'd spent years studying the Bible and all its translations. I pulled out the Bible I had brought along and began to compare their translation with mine. To my surprise, everything seemed to check out.

When the time came for people to go forward to receive Communion, I jumped at the chance to go forward. I glanced at my classmates to see if they were coming too, but their horrified faces told me I was on my own. As I got into line I looked around at all the people there and kept thinking to myself over and over, *These are Christians too . . . these are my brothers and sisters in Christ,* as though willing myself to believe what my professor had told me. I figured if I took Communion with them, perhaps I'd start to believe it for myself.

When I got up front I noticed that the priest and another person were giving out Communion to one line, and two other people were giving out Communion to my line. I tried to watch the people in front of me to see what the protocol was, but the way the line was formed I couldn't see a thing, and I certainly didn't want to step out of line and give away the fact that I had no idea what I was doing.

Finally, it was my turn. There was a lady holding a metallic bowl out of which she grabbed a small, circular Communion wafer. "The body of Christ," she said as she held the wafer aloft over the bowl. Because I hadn't been able to see what I was supposed to do, I just winged it. I gave her my biggest smile, reached out to grab the wafer, and said, "Thank you." Immediately I knew I'd made a mistake. The shocked look on the woman's face caused my whole body to begin trembling. I'd messed up. I'd been found out. Unfortunately, when I'm really nervous I become a bit of a fainting goat. My brain goes numb, I can't think straight, and I revert to autopilot. I continued to follow where the woman in front of me had gone, which was to get in line for the wine, while I held the wafer in my now trembling hands.

As she was drinking from the cup, I realized I hadn't yet eaten the wafer! Fearful of giving myself away even more than I already had, I quickly slipped the wafer into the pocket of my jeans. "The blood of Christ," the man said as he handed me a golden-looking goblet. I said "Thank you," just like before, but this guy didn't seem taken aback. I drank a tiny sip of wine and then swiftly returned to my seat. When it seemed like no one was watching—including my classmates—I slipped the wafer out of my pocket. "I'm sorry, Jesus," I said as I discreetly ate the wafer.

That next Monday, our professor asked how our church visits had gone. I raised my hand and regaled the class with the embarrassing tale of my visit to Saint Rita Catholic Church. My professor's face resembled the face of the lady I'd taken the wafer from. He quickly told the class that only Catholics receive Communion at a Catholic church; everyone else can go forward with their arms crossed to receive a blessing. I sunk a little in my chair. I'd done the one thing I wasn't supposed to do at a Catholic mass, and even though I now knew what to do, I told myself I wouldn't have to worry about making the same mistake again since I'd never be going back.

THE BREAD FROM HEAVEN
AND THE FIRST MASS

Why is Communion in a Catholic church so guarded? In the denominations I was raised in, Communion was a memorial of the Last Supper and nothing more. Christ had told us to "do this . . . in memory of me," so that's all we were doing—memorializing what Jesus did long ago—and Communion was open to anyone who was baptized. We always saw it as a unifying meal, bringing together the variety of Jesus-loving Christians out there. So it was considered an affront for a church to be exclusive with Communion.

The Catholic Church is strict about who receives Communion, because we believe that the bread and wine don't simply represent the body and blood of Jesus, but mystically *are* the body and blood of Jesus Christ. I wasn't wrong in thinking of it as a unifying meal, but I was overly simplistic in my understanding of unity.

To receive Communion in a Catholic church, one must be a Catholic. The reason the Church only allows Catholics to receive is because it understands the Eucharist as a sign of unity: unity in regard to the creeds, Church teaching, and most importantly in the belief of Jesus's presence in the Eucharist. Now, as full as my heart was in its desire for unity with the Catholics at Saint Rita that evening, if I had been honest with myself I would have admitted that I disagreed with pretty much everything the Church taught. My desire for unity was only a superficial desire; below the surface I wanted to continue in what I believed, even if it was completely different from the beliefs of the Catholics I joined for Communion. What I saw as just a little wafer and a glass of wine was in fact Jesus; and my innocent participation in receiving Communion was a failure, as the apostle Paul says to the Corinthians, "to discern the body"—what I've come to see as an act of sacrilegious blasphemy.

It's for this reason the Catholic Church teaches that in order to take Communion, an individual must be properly prepared. For Catholics, this means you need to either abstain from mortal sin or go to confession if you've committed mortal sin. Mortal sin breaks our relationship with Christ, so that relationship needs to be restored in order for us to participate in an act as intimate as Communion. As much as I valued going to Communion, if you had told me back then that it was Jesus's true body and blood, I would have thought you were crazy. I misunderstood a great deal about Catholic teachings, but especially on this topic. When I initially learned what they believed about the Eucharist, I was surprised that I'd always heard more about Catholics "worshipping" Mary and the saints than about them teaching that Jesus is completely and physically present in what looks like a cracker.

This is where Catholic theology is understandably difficult. And you should know that the difficulty isn't new: people have taken issue with Christ's teaching on this since He first spoke about it, which is recorded in the Gospel of John.

Jesus had performed a miraculous sign, feeding thousands of people by multiplying just a couple of loaves of bread. The following day, the crowds came back, seeking more free food. In response, Jesus told them to seek after the bread of life rather than temporary, earthly bread. They asked for the bread of life He described, and He replied, "I am the bread of life; whoever comes to me will never hunger, and whoever believes in me will never thirst" (John 6:35, NABRE).

Even though His words were met with skepticism, He took it a few steps further, connecting himself to the ancient Israelite experience of receiving bread from heaven after their flight from slavery in Egypt:

"Amen, amen, I say to you, whoever believes has eternal life. I am the bread of life. Your ancestors ate the manna in the desert, but they died; this is the bread that comes down from heaven so that one may eat it and not die. I am the living bread that came down from heaven; whoever eats this bread will live forever; and the bread that I will give is my flesh for the life of the world." (John 6: 47–51, NABRE)

Jesus was known to speak in parables, and when He did He'd usually explain His meaning afterward, either to the people or to His disciples. But this time He does neither, and in fact He drives home the point that He is the bread of life that brings eternal life, and that in order to receive this eternal life one needs to eat His flesh, which is in the form of bread, and to partake of His blood, which is in the form of wine. The Gospel of John tells us that people stopped following Him because of this teaching.

Jesus doesn't refer to himself as bread again until the Last Supper as they're celebrating the Passover meal, calling the bread and wine of the meal His body and blood, given and poured out for us. In the Catholic Church, the Last Supper is also known as the first Mass—the institution of the Eucharist. It is during the Last Supper that Jesus teaches His disciples how to celebrate the Mass, and it is the first time Jesus's body, the spotless Lamb of God, is consumed in the form of bread.

Everything that happens in Catholic worship, known as the Mass, culminates in the priest, acting on Christ's behalf, inviting us to participate in the moment Christ died on the cross for our sins as our sacrificial lamb, giving himself to us as the bread of life.

If you're thinking that sounds creepy, you wouldn't be alone. Many people over the last two thousand years have even accused Catholics of being cannibals. However, there is much more going on than just consuming flesh or blood. Because Christ's soul and divinity are present as well, and He is not dead but very much alive, the act of consuming Jesus's body, blood, soul, and divinity in what looks like a piece of bread and a sip of wine is less an act of consumption, and more a physical union with Christ. Much like a bride and groom become physically one flesh, so Christ gives himself to us completely.

When we receive Communion, Jesus is alive in us and He changes us from the inside out. We also physically take Jesus with us into the world. In fact, the word "Mass" comes from the Latin translation of the closing words of the Catholic liturgy: *Ite Missa Est,* which means "Go, it is the dismissal." The Mass is more than a ceremony or service, but the beginning of a mission to take Jesus into the world.

Because of the reality of Christ in that wafer, often referred to as the Blessed Sacrament, religious communities will orient entire days not only on prayer but on attending Mass and receiving the Eucharist. My own community does this—not only as a way to grow more intimately with Christ in our own lives and as a community, but also to aid us in bringing Him to the world.

Attendance at daily mass isn't exclusive to sisters, brothers, monks, and nuns. Many average Catholics will rework their own daily schedule in order to attend Mass. Every day at Mass they listen to Scripture being read, spend time in prayer, are physically united with Christ, and are properly prepared to be sent out to perform the unique tasks the Lord has given them for that day.

"OH THERE YOU ARE, JESUS . . ."

For the longest time I had difficulty believing the Eucharist is the body, blood, soul, and divinity of Jesus. Intellectually it all made sense, so much so that I could argue from Scripture that the Eucharist was Jesus: the manna from heaven. But after years of following Jesus and only ever seeing Him in my mind's eye, my heart seemed to refuse that this piece of bread was actually the love of my life, whom I had known as long as I could remember.

I asked for Jesus's help, of course. "Lord, if that is really You, please help me to see. I understand, but help me to believe . . ." He answered my prayer slowly over the course of several months.

The first thing Jesus did was help me to see Him at Mass. I had been invited to attend a Low Latin Mass, which is an ancient form of the Mass that's celebrated by a priest who whispers the prayers in Latin, making the experience almost completely silent for those of us in the pews. I was used to vibrant and lively church services at my Protestant church, so I didn't expect to have a very good experience at this old quiet version of Mass.

I was handed a red booklet with the Latin words and English translation side-by-side. Since I couldn't hear anything, I couldn't follow along, so I set it aside and just watched. I prayed while I watched the silent choreography of the priest and the server moving around the altar: "Jesus, are You actually in the Catholic Church? I mean, what is even going on here?"

Unexpectedly, I began to see something happening beyond what my eyes could perceive. As the priest stood there praying and bowing to the altar, I also saw Christ praying in the garden of Gethsemane on the night He was arrested. As He continued his silent prayers, I saw Christ before Pilate and the people crying out for His crucifixion—and the priest even turned to wash his hands. I saw Christ being beaten and carrying His cross to be crucified. Suddenly, as little bells were ringing and the priest was raising up the wafer over his head for all to see, I saw Christ dying on the cross.

Tears sprang to my eyes. I couldn't believe what I was seeing, and I was overcome with beauty, awe, and reverence.

The priest continued his prayers and received Communion himself. As he did, I saw Christ in heaven, presenting God with His pure and spotless sacrifice. Then the priest turned to the congregation, descended the steps of the altar, and brought Communion. As he did this, I saw Christ bringing salvation to the people by giving them His own body.

I was stunned. I hadn't understood anything that was going on, and at the same time I felt like I miraculously knew everything that was going on. Later that day I recounted my experience to two priests I'd been getting to know, Father Luan and Father Mark. As I did, their jaws dropped open in shock. They both told me that was exactly what was happening at the Mass.

I was able to accept that Jesus was at Mass now, and I was even beginning to believe He might really be present in that little wafer, but my heart still struggled to completely believe that it was Him. I would pray about it often, and sometimes find myself just staring at the Eucharist expecting for it to transform before my eyes into His face. None of that happened, so I continued to pray and wrestle with this teaching of the Catholic Church.

What turned the tide was a simple conversation I had with the Lord on my way to work.

I was in the middle of my morning commute when I passed by a Catholic church. I pondered my Catholic friends who would make the sign of the cross as they passed Catholic churches, in honor of Jesus being physically present in the church. I rolled my eyes. "Jesus, they seem stuck on You being in there, but I don't see the big deal. I mean, I'm talking to You right now, am I not? In fact, I've talked to You like this for years. I don't have to go to a church to talk to You or know that You're with me."

"True," I heard deep in my heart. Jesus had entered the chat. *"Our relationship is much like a long-distance relationship between a husband and wife who are always connected*

and in constant communication. Though, how much more beautiful is their relationship when they are face-to-face?"

I was stunned into silence yet again. *When I'm near the Eucharist I'm near Christ? Really?* My heart leapt in my chest. I was one step closer to believing that wafer was Jesus.

The final straw isn't much to write about. A few weeks later, I was sitting in an empty church waiting for Mass to begin. I reflected on everything the Lord had been showing me about the Eucharist and all that I had learned, when suddenly I just knew it was Him. All doubt had disappeared from my heart and mind: The Eucharist was Jesus . . . and Jesus was the Eucharist.

I felt like the little Lost Boy in the movie *Hook* as he's searching the face of the grown-up Peter Pan, played by Robin Williams. The boy stares intently as he pushes back Peter Pan's wrinkles, smooshes his cheeks together, and stretches his forehead. Suddenly his eyes light up and a smile stretches across his face. "Oh, there you are, Peter!" he whispers confidently as the other Lost Boys rush in to see Peter for themselves.

In that moment my eyes lit up and a smile spread across my face. "Oh, there You are, Jesus," I whispered in that quiet church. I was face-to-face with my love.

MY FIRST COMMUNION

I was received into the Catholic Church on November 22, 2015, during Sunday Mass on the Feast of Christ the King.

Everything that happened leading up to Mass that morning made me feel like I was in a fairy tale. On the way to Mass my Protestant roommate, Whitney, and I sang along with the *Sister Act* soundtrack as we drove through an unusually magical-looking layer of fog that had wrapped itself around the Saint Johns Bridge. As I walked up the front steps of the church, a small flock of birds flew out of the fountain right in front of me. I turned to Whitney, who confirmed what I was feeling: "You looked like a Disney princess just then," she said.

The Mass itself was beautiful. My friends from vespers, who all attended different parishes in the area, had secretly been practicing with the choir at my parish. They all surprised me by showing up to sing that morning. Several of my Protestant friends who had challenged me along the way—asking me tough questions and listening to me as I worked through all my doubts and fears—also came to the Mass, which touched me more than I could express. That evening, my Catholic friends had a big party for me, not only because I'd just become Catholic but also because my birthday was the very next day! During the party, one of these dear friends began to play the piano in the church hall, unaware that the tune he chose had been my favorite since I was a small child. I looked around the room, overwhelmed with the many gifts the Lord had given me that day. But of all those gifts, the Eucharist was my favorite.

At Mass it's common for worshippers to quietly declare, "My Lord and my God" when the priest raises the consecrated host above his head. I began doing the same thing that morning, but with my own heartfelt twist. I wanted to always remember the union with Christ I would experience every time I received the Eucharist. As the priest held the Eucharist above his head, I looked up and in my heart exclaimed, *My Lord, My God, My Beloved.*

CHAPTER 5

What Is Prayer?

Deus in adiutorium meum intende. Domine ad adiuvandum me festina . . .
O God, come to my assistance. O Lord, make haste to help me . . .

—Opening prayer of the Liturgy of
the Hours (Psalm 70:1)

PIOUS ASSUMPTIONS

I was so anxious the first time I was invited to pray with a bunch of Catholics. I had no idea what I was getting myself into. I showed up early to Saint Birgitta's Catholic Church and sat in my car as I mustered the courage to go in. I had been told that they didn't pray together in the main church, but in a little chapel attached to the rectory, where the priest lived. I watched as unfamiliar faces walked in the side door of a building that looked more like a home for offices than for a priest. When I finally saw a familiar face, I got out of my car and went inside.

The door everyone had entered led straight into the side of the chapel. I was greeted by CJ, whom I'd met a few months prior: the leader of this prayer group. He handed me two hardback books and led me over to a pew. He explained that the large book in English was used to pray vespers, also known as evening prayer, and the small book in Latin was used to pray compline, or night prayer. I was super confused. How did we use books to pray? Nearly every prayer meeting I'd ever been to involved a group of people sitting around with heads bowed, eyes closed, just talking to God about the needs in their lives and the lives of others. But books?

A tall, young, slender priest in a long black robe came in and sat down a couple pews in front of us. I'd only ever seen priests wear cassocks in movies, so I couldn't take my eyes off this new phenomenon, also known as Father Mark. Another priest came in and sat on a pew up front. This was Father Luan, a Vietnamese priest affectionately referred to by the group as Padre. Father Luan wore black slacks and a black clerical shirt with a slightly undone white collar.

Everyone else in the room was about the same age—late twenties, early thirties—and all of them were Catholic and knew what to do. My cheeks flushed as I realized I was the only non-Catholic in the room and didn't know what I was doing. Suddenly Father Luan stood up and everyone followed suit: our prayer meeting had begun. "O God, come to my assistance," he prayed, and everyone replied, "O Lord, make haste to help me."

I followed along in the first large book as this group of young adults and two priests chanted psalms back and forth to each other. Here I was with a bunch of Catholics who were chanting Bible verses. I was shocked! All the Catholics I'd known seemed illiterate when it came to Scripture, yet here I was with a group that was *praying* Scripture. And doing so in a way that was both beautiful and peaceful. What we were calling "prayer" actually seemed more like worship as we proclaimed truths about God from Scripture itself.

And then we were joined by a new voice from the back of the room.

Father Luan's cat, Mr. Walker, had found the chapel door ajar and decided to join us for prayers. The clear sound of a cat's meow mingled with the human voices solemnly chanting the psalms. As everyone realized what was happening, their voices faded as they struggled to stifle their laughter until it could no longer be contained. Everyone was laughing. I watched as Father Mark wrapped his arms around his sides and rolled onto the floor. Our solemn time of prayer had been interrupted, but the only person in the room not laughing was me. I sat in silent shock.

After this little group of Catholics calmed down, we started up where we had left off and finished our prayers. I continued to follow along, all the while still astonished by what had happened. I had assumed, because of the solemnity with which we prayed, that these prayers weren't genuine, weren't real; that everyone was just going through the motions of an ancient religion. The evening had been beautiful, but until Mr. Walker showed up, it had seemed to solidify what I'd always believed about Catholics: They're all about ritual, so they lack heart and humanity in how they worship. Mr. Walker, and the reaction of everyone in the room, had destroyed my assumptions in a heartbeat.

I expected rigid reverence as they recited their prayers. What I found was an odd mix of reverence and intimacy. They were very formal when chanting their prayers, but when they unashamedly burst into laughter I saw a beautiful intimacy as well. I got the impression that, even though their formal prayers had been paused, in their laughter they were still praying. I was confused, intrigued, and I wanted to know more.

WHAT IS PRAYER?

How was it that Catholics could treat both Scripture and laughter as prayer? In the Protestant context, prayer was easily understood as a conversation with God. That conversation could be as casual or as formal as you wanted, though casual was the norm I was used to.

The first thing I needed to understand was how Catholics used the word "prayer." In the Christian tradition I was raised in, prayer was equal to worship, so it made sense that I would be offended by Catholics praying to saints. From my perspective, they were worshipping everyone they prayed to. Even one of the definitions of "pray" in English means to address a reverent petition to a deity.

However, Catholics understand the word "pray" to mean the same thing as its Latin root word, *precari,* which means "to entreat." *Precari* doesn't make a distinction about *who* you are entreating. So, substituting the word "entreat" for the word "pray" is a more accurate way to understand how Catholics pray: Catholics entreat each other for prayer, they entreat Mary for prayer, they entreat the saints for prayer, and they entreat God to attend to their needs.

PRAYER AND THE SAINTS

Once I understood the distinction between how Catholics understand prayer and how I had always understood prayer, I still had an issue with the fact that they were "entreating" a bunch of dead people. What could dead people even do? I mean, they were dead, and I wasn't about to try talking to a bunch of dead humans, no matter how good they were in this life.

Catholics take Jesus's words seriously when He says that whosoever believes in Him "might not perish but might have eternal life" (John 3:16, NABRE). I'd taken those words seriously as well, but hadn't given much thought to what they meant for those who had died, other than that they were in heaven. In fact, I'd imagined heaven was like some other dimension—unconnected from the world we live in. Jesus could go back and forth between us and heaven, but everyone else in heaven was in the dark about what was happening here on earth just like we were in the dark about what was going on with them.

According to Catholic teaching, when someone's body

dies their soul lives on in either purgatory, heaven, or hell. The souls in hell have rejected the offer of eternal life with God and were granted their request to be separated from Him; they are experiencing the torment of their choice. However, those who have accepted God's gift of salvation and eternal life are either in purgatory or in heaven.

The souls in purgatory are on their way to heaven, but they are being refined of any remaining attachment to sin they still had when they died. So we can pray for them—that their refinement is quick, and that they're permitted to enter heaven soon—but the souls in purgatory are in no position to pray for us.

Those who have gone straight to heaven after death, and those who have completed their time in purgatory and are now in heaven, are very much alive and aware of what's going on here on earth. They aren't in another dimension or somehow unaware of our lives here. In fact, they care so much about our lives that they pray for us. After all, they've been in our shoes. They know how hard life is, and they want to continue to support us in any way they can. So, since they aren't burdened with a nine-to-five job, bills, family and friends to take care of, etc., they spend their time in heaven worshipping God and interceding for us.

I was starting to understand the Catholic use of the word "prayer" and the way they viewed the saints, but I still had another hang-up. Why would Catholics talk to the saints instead of just talking to God? Did they think that they couldn't talk directly to God?

I actually didn't have to seek out my Catholic friends for an answer to those questions. I can recall getting myself all worked up thinking about Catholics asking the saints for prayer instead of talking to God about what they wanted, when out of the blue a question interrupted my thoughts: *"Why do you ask your friends for prayer first before talking to Me?"*

I've learned through the years that when my thoughts are interrupted by a question or statement that is contrary to my current line of thinking, it tends to be from God. These statements and questions, as infrequent as they are, bring truth and clarity to my jumbled thoughts.

I hadn't considered that asking the saints for prayer was like asking my friends for prayer. But it was true. I'd often run to my friends and ask for their prayers before talking to God. It never crossed my mind that I *couldn't* talk to God first, but in my humanity I felt more comfortable talking—and usually also complaining—to another human about my problems. I mean, if my problems were at all my fault, I knew that in talking to God I'd eventually have to do something about them; but in talking to another person I could freely vent to someone who would commiserate with me more than convict me. Catholics asking the saints for prayer began to make more sense: They didn't talk to them in lieu of talking to God, but in addition to talking to God.

I recently found a piece of art on Instagram that illustrates this realization I arrived at all those years ago. Talking to the saints and Mary wouldn't keep me from talking to God any more than talking to my friends and family. They aren't mutually exclusive. Mary and the saints would just be added to the list of people I'd ask to pray for me.

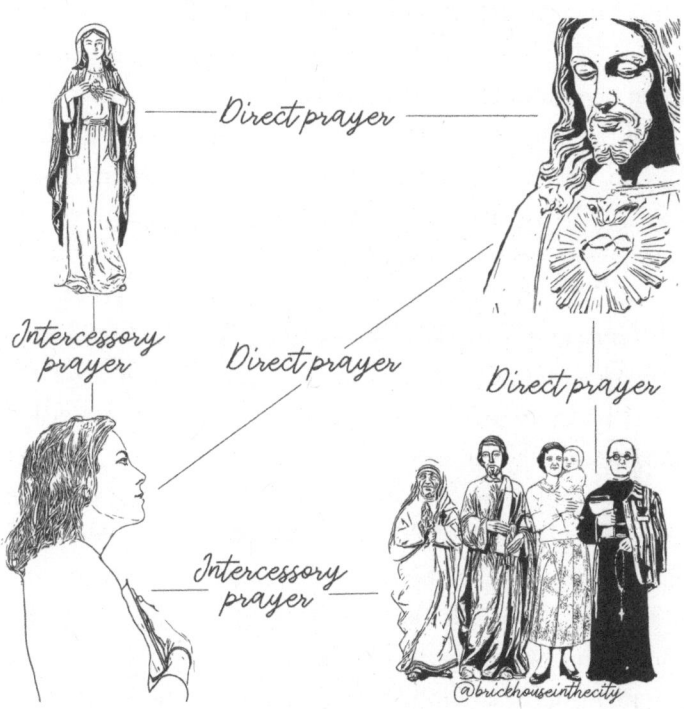

@brickhouseinthecity

Understanding how Catholics "pray" to the saints had been my biggest concern and stumbling block in learning about Catholicism. However, once I understood that entreating the saints was no different than asking my mom, a church friend, or a bunch of strangers on the internet for prayer, I was able to start learning more about the variety of ways that Catholics pray to God.

OFFERING IT UP

I'd heard the phrase "offer it up" tossed around among the Catholics I knew whenever someone was complaining about any difficulty they were having. The way they used the phrase implied that they were referring to prayer, which I could not seem to wrap my mind around. I mean, what was "it"? What did it mean to offer "it" up? And what did that have to do with prayer?

For Catholics, prayer goes beyond words. Prayer has substance and even a physicality to it. This idea of prayer as a physical offering appears in the earliest chapters of the Bible, where sacrifice is a form of prayer in which physical objects were offered to God during worship.

A modern version of this sacrificial offering of prayer is seen in the lighting of candles in a Catholic church. An offering or sacrifice in the form of a monetary donation (for the cost of the candle) is given; then the candle is lit with a particular prayer request in mind. That prayer is then consistently offered to God for as long as the candle burns.

We also see this physical act of offering in the New Testament in Jesus's sacrificial death for us on the cross. He acts as our example of what a physical act of prayer looks like, and, just like in the Old Testament, this type of prayer is also sacrificial. Saint Paul describes this new, personal sacrifice in his letter to the Church of Rome when he urges the believers there to "offer your bodies as a living sacrifice, holy and pleasing to God, your spiritual worship" (Romans 12:1).

Catholics take the sacrifice of their bodies very seriously. They treat all their suffering—whether self-inflicted, imposed, accidental, unintentional, etc.—as an offering that can be made to God as a physical and sacrificial prayer.

I tried this out one evening as I was on my way home from church. We had just received a huge fall of snow, so I opted to take the bus. As I was waiting at the bus stop, despite all my layers and wool socks, I could feel the cold taking over my fingers and toes. Each breeze felt like pins and needles on my exposed face. I checked the bus's location on my phone app and discovered I'd be waiting for another thirty minutes.

I didn't want to pass the time by looking at my phone, and so, with nothing else to distract myself, I began to focus on every bit of my increasing pain. I turned my thoughts instead to what I was going home to: my nice warm house, my warm and cuddly dog, some hot soup for dinner. As I thought about these comforts, I remembered there were people enduring this same cold who had no warm comforts to look forward to. Our city had a sizable homeless population, so the reality was that lots of folks were going to sleep in the very cold I was so desperate to flee.

I decided to "offer up" my discomfort. I asked the Lord for my pain to be a prayer for all those who were going to be suffering in the cold much longer than I would be that evening. Anytime I found my mind wandering back to the pain, I'd turn my thoughts back to prayer.

This act of offering my suffering as a prayer had an amazing effect on me. The pain in my body was no longer an affliction to be endured, but a gift to be offered for others. As I reflected on those who were suffering more than I was, I found myself humbled and grateful for the comforts in my life. Of course, I'll possibly never know how my prayers may have helped those I was offering the pain for, but I was also grateful for the chance to pray for them. Offering up my pain turned my mind from selfish thoughts of my discomfort to selfless thoughts of the needs of others.

REPETITIVE PRAYER

A Catholic's prayers aren't only physical, but repetitive as well. Again, this is one of the issues I had with Catholics: How can a repeated prayer be heartfelt?

When I was little, my favorite way to pray was lying in bed at night and talking to God as though He was in the room with me. I'd tell Him about my day, the things that made me happy, the things I was upset about, and the people I wanted to pray for. I surprised my mom one evening when she could hear me talking through my bedroom door. Popping her head into my room, she asked, "Who are you talking to?" Her eyes widened as I told her I was talking to God. She smiled, encouraged me to continue, and shut the door.

These times talking with God were deeply personal and intimate, so when I learned that Catholics repeated a lot of memorized prayers I saw this, in comparison to my own experience, as cold, lacking emotion, and devoid of intimacy. To put it bluntly, the idea of praying anything pre-written repulsed me. I wanted my words to Christ to be based on how I was feeling in the moment, not confined to someone else's scripted prayer.

What I didn't see at the time was the potential danger in always basing my prayers on how I was feeling. As my emotions grew in intensity with age, I found myself falling into a solo echo chamber. My conversations with God were beautiful and honest, but when I was going through a difficult season, I could get stuck in a rut of just talking about myself all the time. God became no more than a sounding board for my pity party. In addition to that, if I didn't feel any sort of consolation or comfort in my prayers to God, I would start to think He wasn't listening, He didn't care, or He had left me. These feelings would only worsen my already miserable feelings.

I fell into this negative prayer cycle once when I was having trouble with a coworker. He had been put in charge of an event that had to do with Catholicism, and, as I was the only Catholic on the Protestant Christian college campus we worked at, he asked my advice. I was excited to help and offered all the insight and advice I could. As the time of the event neared, I discovered that he hadn't used any of my input and instead had just created the event based on his own ideas of Catholicism.

I wasn't only livid; I was offended, hurt, and confused. Every time I'd pray about the situation, tears of anger would stream down my face. I hadn't been listened to, even though I was consulted and was more of an expert on the topic than my coworker. I'd ask God for help but found my prayers turning quickly to venting and crying.

Around this same time, I discovered the Litany of Humility. After one read-through I was struck by the truth of the prayers, as well as their difficulty. They were both comforting and convicting—especially the line asking for deliverance from "the desire of being consulted." So, for the next month, every morning as I began my day at work, with a deep breath I would pray the Litany of Humility.

In doing so, I found my anger fading, and I began to see the pride behind it as well. I also found that other lines in the litany would stick out to me, depending on what I was going through that day. As I prayed these simple words, my heart began to change.

THE LITANY OF HUMILITY

O Jesus! Meek and humble of heart, Hear me.
From the desire of being esteemed, Deliver me, Jesus.
From the desire of being loved, Deliver me, Jesus.
From the desire of being extolled, Deliver me, Jesus.
From the desire of being honored, Deliver me, Jesus.
From the desire of being praised, Deliver me, Jesus.
From the desire of being preferred, Deliver me, Jesus.
From the desire of being consulted, Deliver me, Jesus.
From the desire of being approved, Deliver me, Jesus.
From the fear of being humiliated, Deliver me, Jesus.
From the fear of being despised, Deliver me, Jesus.
From the fear of suffering rebukes, Deliver me, Jesus.

From the fear of being calumniated, Deliver me, Jesus.

From the fear of being forgotten, Deliver me, Jesus.

From the fear of being ridiculed, Deliver me, Jesus.

From the fear of being wronged, Deliver me, Jesus.

From the fear of being suspected, Deliver me, Jesus.

That others may be loved more than I, Jesus, grant me the grace to desire it.

That others may be esteemed more than I, Jesus, grant me the grace to desire it.

That in the opinion of the world, others may increase and I may decrease, Jesus, grant me the grace to desire it.

That others may be chosen and I set aside, Jesus, grant me the grace to desire it.

That others may be praised and I unnoticed, Jesus, grant me the grace to desire it.

That others may be preferred to me in everything, Jesus, grant me the grace to desire it.

That others become holier than I, provided that I may become as holy as I should, Jesus, grant me the grace to desire it.

—(Litany of Humility, The Original
Pieta Prayer Book)

After my experience with the Litany of Humility, I wondered if there were other prayers out there that might have a similar effect when prayed. I prayed the Litany of Trust and it convicted me of doubts I was having. I prayed the Rosary (see Chapter 6) and saw Christ's life in the world around me. I prayed the Our Father and pondered whether

I was forgiving others, and if I was seeking God's will to be done in my life.

These written prayers not only matched how I was feeling at the time, but they spoke truth into those feelings as I prayed, changing my heart in the process. I still spoke freely to God throughout my day, but I began to include prayers that not only helped me express how I was feeling, but also challenged and refined me.

LITURGY OF THE HOURS

The average Catholic may only be slightly familiar with them, but the Liturgy of the Hours are the common prayers of all Catholic priests, deacons, monks, brothers, nuns, religious sisters, and other consecrated individuals. However, there are a lot of Catholics who enjoy praying some, or even all, of the Liturgy of the Hours as well. That's how I ended up praying vespers and compline with a couple of priests, some young adult Catholics, and a cat at the beginning of this chapter.

I'd always been inspired by the life of service lived by sisters and nuns, but had been ignorant of what their prayers looked like up until that first time praying vespers. After that night of prayer, I was hooked. I loved the use of Scripture as prayer, the beauty of the chant, and the intimacy that seemed present in something so formal. I came back week after week to join them for prayers on Sundays. During the week I'd find videos online of common parts of the Liturgy of the Hours, so that I could practice. I started praying compline (night prayer) on my own from time to time.

I learned that for those who pray all the hours, of which there are up to eight, they do so at set times throughout the day, and build the rest of their day around these times of prayer. Each prayer doesn't take an hour to recite, but consecrates that hour. Stopping to pray throughout the day ensures that one is "praying constantly," and that the entire day itself is consecrated in prayer. I'd drive to a local Benedictine monastery and join the monks for prayer from time to time. I loved that these prayers were something I could participate in as a non-Catholic, and that they were also connecting me to those living religious life—a group I'd always been intrigued by.

Years later, I can see how the Lord was foreshadowing my call to be a sister—even down to Mr. Walker's musical meows. As reverent as we are when we pray together, the brothers live on a farm, and the animals have been known to join in—our cows, Bubbles and Buttercup, are the biggest repeat offenders. To clarify, Buttercup is a gluttonous free spirit who likes to jump out of their fenced area and go digging around for snacks in the shed where we keep all the animal feed. Whenever Buttercup goes on her food-seeking adventures, Bubbles sounds the alarm to let us know, and she's so loud that we can hear her in the church where we pray.

A unique aspect of praying these hours is that they are meant to be prayed with others. The prayers are broken down into sections meant to be chanted or recited back and forth between two groups of people. Since I'm currently the only woman in my community, I usually get to experience this conversation-like experience only when I join the brothers for prayer.

Prayer begins with the leader breaking the silence of the church: *Deus in adiutorium meum intende* (O God, come to my assistance). As though both answering his prayer and echoing it, the rest of the community replies: *Domine ad adiuvandum me festina* (O Lord, make haste to help me). Then we all join together: *Gloria Patri, et Filio, et Spiritui Sancto, Sicut erat in principio, et nunc, et semper, et in sæcula sæculorum. Amen.* (Glory be to the Father, and to the Son, and to the Holy Spirit. As it was in the beginning, is now, and ever shall be, world without end. Amen.)

On and on, our prayers continue as we both cry out to God as well as remember His faithfulness. During our prayers we bring with us not only our own concerns and struggles, but the prayer requests and intentions of others. After all, the life of a religious is not meant to be self-centered, but a life of service for others—and the number one service we offer is prayer.

SOUND OF SILENCE

I went on a silent retreat two months before I became Catholic. As an extremely talkative person, I was intrigued with the idea of not talking for a period of time. And since

I like a good challenge, I signed up. I quickly found not talking easy, mainly because no one else was talking either, so I didn't feel rude ignoring others and getting lost in my thoughts.

What I had a hard time getting used to was how noisy my thoughts were. I journaled to try to relieve the seemingly nonstop chatter, and even took a couple naps. After a day, the initial chatter in my mind quieted down and I was able to think more clearly. I noticed trends: things I thought about a lot, things I didn't think about enough, and even thought patterns that led me to sinful actions. This silence was eye-opening and convicting, like cleaning out an old closet; I was able to see what I needed to keep, what I needed to get rid of, and how to better organize my thoughts.

Not only was the silence helping me face the messes in my life I'd avoided because they seemed too overwhelming, but I was also able to listen more closely to the voice of God and see His presence in my life.

During this silent retreat I became enamored with a life-sized statue of Christ that I kept passing on my way to and from my room. I'd stop in front of it and imagine what it would be like to have Christ sitting in front of me, or what it might have been like to stand in front of Him in the midst of His torture and agony. This statue stimulated my thoughts and imagination, and aided my reflections that weekend. I knew it wasn't Christ, but I longed to be as physically close to Him as I was to that statue.

Where I did meet Christ on that retreat was during a

time of Adoration. I'd been to Adoration at Catholic churches before, but I was still struggling with the concept. During Adoration a Communion wafer that has been consecrated at Mass, and is now the body of Jesus, is displayed in an ornate holder called a monstrance. Since the wafer has all the appearance of bread, it can look like Catholics worship crackers, though in reality they are face-to-face with Jesus.

I wrestled with my doubts as I sat with my eyes closed in the silence of the chapel with the Blessed Sacrament exposed on the altar. Was Jesus really physically here with me? I suddenly had an overwhelming feeling that I wasn't alone. I felt that I had someone sitting on either side of me. On my right was Jesus, and on my left was Mary. I continued to sit there with my eyes closed. I was convinced that if I opened my eyes I wouldn't see anyone there, but the feeling that I wasn't alone was so tangible that I began to wonder if they might actually be there when I opened my eyes. Jesus spoke to my heart. He knew my desire to be close to Him, and He wanted me to know that He always was close, whether I could see Him or not, and whether I could feel His presence or not. In the silence, with all distractions gone, I was able to let the Lord love me.

All these types of prayer we've covered so far have something in common: They are directed toward either God, people, or both at the same time. However, a large part of prayer is silence and contemplation. In these periods of silence we are able to reflect on our lives, our struggles, our sins, the lives of the saints, the life of Christ, and the life of

Mary. While uncomfortable for many in our very noisy society, silence is a necessary part of our spiritual growth.

Even if our society weren't full of noise, our minds certainly would be. We are addicted to filling the noise any way we can: phones, music, people, video games, drinking, books, drugs, games, food, social media, porn, TV shows, movies, the list goes on and on. What is it we are trying to avoid hearing or looking at? Nothing as imaginative as you'd see in a horror movie. No, what we avoid is reflecting on our humanity: regrets, mistakes, sins, pain, loss, death, etc. In silence, reality becomes loud and difficult to ignore.

However, if we are surrounded by noise, we also drown out the voice of a God who loves us more than we can imagine. And perhaps that's the scariest thing of all. Great love often brings with it great pain: You see it in all the greatest romantic movies. How much more real is that pain when you know that a perfect God loves an imperfect you?

If prayer is a conversation, then what I learned in silence is to make sure I'm not the only one talking in that conversation. Silence allows me to listen—listen to what I'm struggling with in my heart, listen to the changes that need to be made, and most importantly, listen to what God is trying to tell me. Sometimes, even more than venting out my needs or reciting another Hail Mary, the thing I need most in prayer is to allow God to speak.

Mental prayer in my opinion is nothing else than an intimate sharing between friends; it means taking time frequently to be alone with Him who we know loves us. The important thing is not to think much but to love much and so do that which best stirs you to love. Love is not great delight but desire to please God in everything.

—Saint Teresa of Ávila

CHAPTER 6

Who Is the Virgin Mary?

A ROCKY RELATIONSHIP

Before becoming a Catholic, my feelings about the Virgin Mary were complicated. I hadn't always been a fan of the mother of Jesus, though I wouldn't go so far as to say that I hated her. During the thirty-four years of my life as a Protestant, before becoming Catholic, discussions of Mary were mostly confined to Christmas sermons and nothing more. As a child, I was chosen to portray her in a Christmas play—and I LOVED IT. I clearly remember wearing a blue and white "Bible costume" my grandma made, holding a baby doll, and pretending that he was Jesus and I was his mom.

As a teenager, I respected Mary's poise, self-control, and strength when reading Luke 2:19: "But Mary treasured up all these things and pondered them in her heart" (NIV). Here she was at the Nativity, having just given birth to the

Messiah, surrounded by a bunch of shepherds who had been directed by a ton of angels to come visit her new son. If I were her, I would have been quick to tell everyone with a pulse about everything that had just happened. But Mary didn't. She treasured everything in her heart. There was a lot I could learn from her in that one verse.

As an adult, I found myself increasingly torn between my youthful respect for her and fear of what I perceived as worship of her. On a business trip in California, I encountered a giant steel statue of Mary in a park. Each morning before our conference, a coworker and I ate breakfast next to the statue. We watched folks show up after Mass and lay flowers at her feet. I felt bad for those people. They seemed so confused, I thought, and I prayed they would turn from their idolatrous ways.

Standing next to the 32-foot tall steel statue of Mary at Our Lady of Peace Catholic Church in Santa Clara, California

By the time I hit my thirties, that fear of Mary worship had turned to jealousy and anger. My boyfriend at the time began to embrace the Catholic Church, and with it—*her*. We were both Protestants, but he spoke openly about his newfound Catholic thoughts. He shared his experiences praying the Rosary or asking Mary for prayer. Every time he mentioned her name, jealousy boiled up inside of me. I was no longer a fan of the mother of our Lord.

So what has changed since then? I mean, I'm writing this now as a Catholic . . . and Catholics tend to like Mary. A lot. Here are some of the main things that took me from anger to admiration of, and devotion to, the Blessed Virgin Mary.

MISUNDERSTANDINGS AND MISCOMMUNICATION

First, I had to confront all of the theological arguments. But in order to engage them sincerely, I had to set aside my feelings of anger and jealousy so I could listen and learn. My initial steps didn't involve the Catholic Church's teachings. Instead, I looked to the Orthodox Church.

I pelted an Orthodox friend of mine with questions on what they believed about Mary. The questions were usually framed as "Catholics believe such-and-such about Mary . . . What say you?" My Orthodox friend usually responded with "Yeah, we pretty much believe that too." It always left me speechless and thoughtful.

I started to realize that much of what I'd grown up be-lieving about Mary wasn't true. That meant eating a big slice of humble pie. I didn't like hearing that I was wrong, especially when I had believed so fiercely that I was right!

Consider those folks laying flowers at the base of the Mary statue. What I viewed as idol worship was, in fact, reverence—akin to placing flowers at the grave of a loved one. However, since Mary doesn't have a proper grave, many believers use photos, icons, or statues as places of memorial.[*]

SHE ALWAYS POINTS US TO JESUS

Mary always points us back to Jesus. This was something I experienced big-time when I was learning to pray the Rosary.

The Rosary is a specific set of prayers that are prayed with accompanying beads. I apologize to all my Protestant friends and family who thought that perhaps I wasn't one of *those* Catholics. Alas, I am. Please allow me to explain.

I didn't start praying the Rosary until *after* I was a Cath-olic. As much as I had learned about the Blessed Mother, I still had a hard time with her. What can I say? Thirty-four

---

[*] Both Catholic and Orthodox traditions hold that Mary was taken phys-ically into heaven (known as the Feast of the Assumption or Dormition of Mary, respectively); in the Catholic Church and some Orthodox churches, the feast day is August 15.

years of mistrust didn't fade easily. But, desperate for the healing of a mother of four at my church who was dying of cancer, I figured I'd give the ol' Rosary a go.

Part of praying the Rosary is thinking about certain aspects of Jesus's life, called "mysteries."

I began to pray fervently for this woman's healing with each Our Father, Hail Mary, and Glory Be, and especially as I reflected on each aspect of Christ's life. But as I worked my way around those beads and through those mysteries, I found my heart changing. I felt the Lord teaching me what it looked like to follow Him, and that sometimes He allows us to suffer just as He suffered. My prayers for this dying woman changed from petitioning for healing, to begging for her to have the strength to endure her trial, just as Christ himself endured his own.

She ended up passing a few months later, and from what I've heard of her final months, weeks, and days on this earth, the Lord answered my prayers for her to have strength. I wouldn't have had that experience in prayer had I not decided to pick up a rosary and give Mary a chance.

AN ACTIVE AND CARING MOTHER

A big question of mine while learning about Mary was whether she would be involved in my life. I had gotten to a place where I respected her, admired her, and theologically understood her, but in my eyes she was still a historical figure: someone who was in heaven but had no tangible effect on my life down here. So I decided to test what a relationship with Jesus's mom looked like: I asked her to pray for me.

My temporary housing was quickly coming to an end, so I needed a new place to live. I had been looking for places all over the area, but everything I liked was snatched up before I finished filling out an application. A duplex with one open unit was available and seemed a perfect fit, and I was hopeful that I had caught this one before anyone else. I happened to show up to the open house at the same time as another gal who was also interested in the property. She was super nice, and we chatted easily as we filled out our applications, even though we both knew that we were vying for the same place. The landlord said he'd look things over and give us a call to let us know his decision.

In my car, I poured my heart out to Jesus: how hard the process of getting a place had been, how stressed I was, how I was running out of time, how nice the other girl was, and how much I wanted that unit. As I was talking to Jesus, I got the impression that I should try asking his mom for prayer.

This attempt was awkward: "Ummm. Hi. Mary? I don't know how to do this. Do I just talk to you like I talk to Jesus? Sheesh, this is uncomfortable. So I guess . . . Could you pray for me to get this apartment? But I feel bad, since that gal wants it too. Hmmm . . . Okay, I'm going to take a chance and ask you for something big. Maybe if you answer it I'll believe you're actually listening. Mary, can you please pray not only for me to get that unit, but that the other unit opens up and that girl can get it, so we can be neighbors?"

I finished praying, and as I drove away I figured nothing would happen. Even if she was up there listening, I was convinced there was no way she'd consent to pray for such a huge request.

The next day I got a call from the landlord. I was accepted! I was so excited and relieved that my search was finally over! Then he asked which unit I wanted. Confused, I asked what he was talking about—I'd only applied for the one vacant unit. He told me that the folks who were supposed to move into the other unit had backed out, leaving open both units of the duplex. He was offering me first pick, and then giving the other unit to the other gal who had applied.

The very specific request I'd asked Mary to pray for had been answered, and completely. Not only was I getting the unit, but that gal I'd met was getting the other unit, and we were going to be neighbors. Once my excitement over this great news settled down, I was sobered, knowing that Mary, the mother of Jesus Christ, had heard me, prayed for me, and that Jesus had answered her request. I didn't understand how it all happened, but I couldn't deny that it had.

What helped was learning that the crucifixion of Christ has a lot to do with how Catholics interact with Mary:

Standing by the cross of Jesus were His mother and His mother's sister, Mary the wife of Clopas, and Mary of Magdala. When Jesus saw His mother and the disciple there whom He loved, He said to his mother, "Woman, behold, your son." Then He said to the disciple, "Behold, your mother." And from that hour the disciple took her into his home. (John 19:25–27, NABRE)

In this moment, Jesus wasn't just entrusting His mother to John, but to all His beloved disciples—including us. In that moment, Mary's ministry of being the mother of Christ expanded to include being the mother of us all. And as a caring mother, alive in heaven, of course she wants to help her children on earth.

TRUST, SACRIFICE, AND THE PIETÀ

The last thing my little journey with Mary taught me: She understands Trust and Sacrifice in ways that I long to emulate.

For years I wrestled with what the Lord had planned for me regarding my vocation. Would I marry? Would I have kids? Would I become a sister or nun? Would I become a consecrated virgin? Would I die before any of that happened, rendering all my questions pointless? God knew, but He was frustratingly silent.

But why was I frustrated? Because, after a lifetime of following Him, I still struggled to trust Him with the big and little details of my life. I wanted to know what the plan was so I could be prepared; instead, He asked me to trust Him with both the plans and the preparation.

And then I thought of Mary.

The Annunciation by Francesco Albani

There is nothing Mary could have done to prepare for the bomb that the angel Gabriel dropped on her. She was not yet married and she was a virgin, but she was going to give birth to a baby? And not just any baby, but the Son of God? But putting aside what must have been overwhelming confusion, she trusted God and opened herself up to His plan. In his painting, Francesco Albani vividly depicts Mary's openness at the moment she chooses to accept the Lord's will for her life.

Michelangelo's *Pietà* is on display at the Vatican in
Rome. I had the opportunity to see it in person during
a pilgrimage in October of 2016. There is also a replica
of the original at the National Sanctuary of our
Sorrowful Mother in Portland, Oregon.

Fast-forward to another depiction of Mary, on the worst
day of her life. I love Michelangelo's sculpture, *Pietà,* for *so*
many reasons. A big one is the positioning of her hands. She
isn't clutching Christ to her chest. She isn't shaking her fist
at God for taking her child. She's holding Him, but still
open. Still offering. This time she's not only offering herself,
but her beloved son as well. While He sacrificed himself in

death, she sacrificed herself through her life. It's the very thing I longed to do, no matter what my vocation would be. I want to live my life in such a way that it is a daily sacrifice for the Lord and for those I love. Mary's story is an example that we can all learn from, no matter our state in life.

Even now, with the peace of knowing my vocation is to serve God by founding a religious order, Mary's abandonment to His will still inspires me. So in those moments when I'm frustrated—when I don't know what I'm doing next, when I feel like life isn't going my way, when I have to let go of something or someone I love, when I suffer a loss, or when I receive an amazing gift—I think of Mary's trust and sacrifice. And I keep my hands open.

THE MANY NAMES OF MARY

Mary is often referred to with a variety of titles and roles. For example, I had no idea that Our Lady of Guadalupe, Our Lady of Fátima, and Our Lady of Lourdes were all names for Mary. I genuinely thought they were three different saints from Guadalupe, Fátima, and Lourdes. However, such titles are given to Mary when she appears to a particular saint or group of people.

As of now, there have been sixteen apparitions recognized by the Catholic Church. While the messages she offers may vary, they are consistent in their overall intent of pointing people to repent and believe in Jesus. These apparitions are often followed by miracles, healings, or other signs showing their validity. Even then, the Church is cautious before confirming that any particular sighting of Mary is valid.

Mary is also given titles that refer to her significant role in the redemption of the world through Jesus. The name *Theotokos* is Greek for "Mother of God," signifying that Jesus was not only born fully human, but also fully God. She's called the New Ark of the Covenant, indicating that she carried in her body the living Word of God in the way that the original Ark carried the written Word of God. She's also called the New Eve; whereas Eve's decision to sin brought about death for all, Mary's decision to carry Jesus brought about life for all.

THE RELATIONSHIP CONTINUES

Mary had been so woven into my journey from the beginning that when I became a Catholic I chose "Mary Thérèse" as my confirmation name, to honor both the Virgin Mary and Saint Thérèse of Lisieux. (Miraculously, my priest let me choose two saints, even though having two confirmation saints is *very* uncommon.)

Even though I chose to take her name at the time, I still wasn't completely comfortable with Mary. But I'm so glad I did. I've grown closer to her since then. She brings a feminine comfort to my faith that I didn't realize I was missing. Mary has redeemed my womanhood, pointed me to Christ, taught me what trust and sacrifice look like, and been a mother to me in some of my darkest moments.

Most recently, I had fallen sick with a bad case of Covid. Quarantined in the convent for weeks during the Christmas season, I consoled myself daily that I wasn't really alone; Jesus and Mary were there with me. I got progressively worse and started to fear the noises my lungs were beginning to make with each breath. I knew whatever was in there needed to come out, but all I could muster was a dry cough. As I stood in the kitchen trying not to despair, I recalled a prayer I had learned some years back:

Remember, O most gracious Virgin Mary, that never was it known that anyone who fled to thy protection, implored thy help, or sought thy intercession was left unaided. Inspired by this confidence, I fly unto thee, O Virgin of virgins, my Mother. To thee do I come, before thee I stand, sinful and sorrowful. O Mother of the Word Incarnate, despise not my petitions, but in thy mercy hear and answer me. Amen.

I had made it through the first sentence of the prayer when I was suddenly struck with the urge to cough. This cough was much different than the dry hacking I'd been used to. I ran to the sink and finally had a productive cough. With tears in my eyes I finished my prayer, even though I knew Mary had already come to my aid. A few days later my fever was gone and my strength began to return.

I had always been afraid that if I loved Mary at all, it would mean that I loved Christ less. But the opposite has proved true. The more I learn about Mary and learn from her, the more I fall in love with her Son. She supports me, encourages me, prays for me, heals me, and inspires me. I find myself wanting to be more like Mary, faithfully pointing others to the wonderful love of Jesus.

Hail, Holy Queen, Mother of Mercy! Our life, our sweetness, and our hope! To thee do we cry, poor banished children of Eve, to thee do we send up our sighs, mourning and weeping in this valley of tears. Turn, then, most gracious advocate, thine eyes of mercy toward us; and after this our exile show unto us the blessed fruit of thy womb Jesus; O clement, O loving, O sweet Virgin Mary. Pray for us, O Holy Mother of God, that we may be made worthy of the promises of Christ. Amen.

CHAPTER 7

Who Are the Saints?

EARLY INSPIRATIONS

O when the saints go marching in,
O when the saints go marching in,
O Lord, I want to be in that number
When the saints go marching in.

I used to sing this song in my Sunday School classes. From about the age of five, when I began grasping that there was a God who loved me, all I wanted was to love Him and live my life for Him: to be one of those saints marching into heaven, after having lived for God on earth. At that wee age, I knew nothing of Catholic saints and the theology they represented. *Who exactly are these saints, and who gets to be a famous one?* was not something I asked. The saints we sang about, were taught about, were simply Christians who faithfully followed Jesus.

My mom's Sunday School teacher, Mrs. Duckworth, was my introduction to this kind of saint. She passed away before I was born, but everyone who had known her loved her for her kind heart, hospitable nature, and helpful attitude. My mom's accolades for this beloved woman made me hope that perhaps someday I could be as well-loved and as holy as she was.

After Mrs. Duckworth, I was introduced to some not-so-local saints: Amy Carmichael and Corrie Ten Boom. An Irish Christian missionary who traveled to India, Amy Carmichael offered refuge to young girls who had fled from lives of temple prostitution. Corrie Ten Boom was a Dutch Christian who with her family hid Jews from the Nazis during World War II. The love these two women felt for Jesus pushed them to love others with so much bravery that their lives were endangered. The practical love of Mrs. Duckworth was inspiring, but I was downright captivated by the courageous love of Amy and Corrie.

Then I discovered Jim Elliot. Along with Nate Saint and three other missionaries, Jim Elliot brought the good news of Jesus's love to a remote village in Ecuador—only to be murdered by the village warriors. But the story didn't end there. Instead of fleeing, Jim's wife, Elisabeth, and Nate's wife, Rachel, pressed forward with the mission their husbands had begun. These strong women not only met with the men who had murdered Jim and Nate, but forgave them.

Stories like these fueled in me a passion to live my faith on that level, like I never had before. Jim Elliot said, "He is no fool who gives what he cannot keep to gain that which he cannot lose." Upon hearing this, I made it my motto. My desire to learn more about Christians who had lived and died for Christ grew fervently; I embraced the stories of these martyrs. I especially loved the book *Jesus Freaks* by DC Talk and Voice of the Martyrs, dog-earing the stories that were especially inspiring to me—people whose love for Jesus was so strong that they were willing to die rather than renounce their faith.

Invigorated by these stories of heroic faith, I longed to do big things for God. I didn't see martyrdom as a likelihood since I didn't live in a country or culture known for killing Christians, but that didn't mean I couldn't still give Him my whole life: future plans, education, jobs, ministries, dreams, home, family, friends—everything. I may not have been able to die for my faith, but I could certainly die to the world in order to live my faith more fully. Little did I know, a hundred years before I was having all of these thoughts and desires, a relatively unknown Catholic nun had had the same heart to follow Jesus.

SAINT THÉRÈSE OF LISIEUX

St. Thérèse of Lisieux—also known as Saint Thérèse of the Child Jesus and the Holy Face, and the Little Flower—was a French Carmelite nun who entered the convent at the unconventional age of fifteen and died from tuberculosis just nine years later in 1897, at the age of twenty-four. When it was discovered that she was nearing the end of her life, she was asked by her superiors to write a book about herself, which she did: *Story of a Soul.*

To be fair, I have to admit that I didn't care for Saint Thérèse when I first learned about her. I had asked a Catholic friend to think of any saints he knew of who would be a good match for me. At the time, I was still Protestant and had no intention of becoming Catholic. I just thought the saints had cool lives, and I wanted to learn more about them. When he suggested Saint Thérèse, she sounded wimpy. Especially with a nickname like "the Little Flower." Blah. Boring. I wanted him to suggest someone like Saint Catherine of Siena, who was bold enough to call out the pope, or Saint Teresa of Ávila, who was passionate and vocal, writing extensively on suffering and admonishing those in the Church who were doing wrong.

Nope. He stuck to his guns: Saint Thérèse. So I ignored his suggestion. (Maturity is one of my strong points.)

Later, as I cautiously started getting interested in becoming Catholic, I asked the same question of another Catholic friend, CJ, who immediately ran and grabbed his copy of *Story of a Soul*. This time, the way he described her piqued my interest. She was a bit stubborn, saw the world simply, emphasized the importance of love in all things, and was unconventional. So far so good! Saint Thérèse was back on the table. I started reading.

Talk about a girl after my own heart! Saint Thérèse was so in love with Jesus that all she wanted to do was to enter the convent and spend her days married to the love of her life. Women were not allowed to do that until they were at least sixteen years old. But she was so set in her desire, she took a trip to Rome with her father and sister. During a public audience, she actually approached the pope himself. She had been specifically told *not* to speak to him. Not only did she speak to him, she tearfully collapsed into his lap and asked him to allow her to enter the convent early. Wow. I read that story and thought, *Girl . . . I would have done the same thing!* The bishop who had the final say ended up granting her permission to enter, a year early.

While in the convent, Thérèse found some of the older nuns difficult to love. But instead of letting it be what it was, she decided to see loving them as sort of a challenge, and she set out to love them even more. She talked often about finding little acts of love to do for others, even if they were a sacrifice for her. No: *especially* if they were a sacrifice for her. For Thérèse, every loving act she performed was not only for the person directly involved, but also for Jesus, the love of her life.

One of my favorite stories she told was when she was helping a fellow sister with the laundry. This was back before washing machines, so helping with the laundry meant rolling up your sleeves and getting your hands wet. As they sat opposite each other, washing away, the other sister kept splashing Thérèse with the dirty water. While initially offended by these little showers, instead of showing her frustration Thérèse decided to embrace them and be happy about it. What was even crazier to me is she didn't do so out of pride or superiority, but out of love for this sister and, most of all, love for God.

As amazing as I found her little stories, the moment I knew Thérèse was my girl was when I read what she wrote about her discontent with being "just a sister," despite all the love and passion she had in her heart for Jesus.

She explained that her discontentment with being a sister wasn't due to something wrong with her state in life, but to her love of all the other vocations out there. She didn't want to only be a sister—she wanted to be a soldier, a doctor of the Church, a priest, a missionary, and even a martyr.

She described how, while desiring to live for Jesus in all these vocations, she happened to read in Scripture where the apostle Paul writes about each of them. In 1 Corinthians 12 he states that no one is called to be everything, but that we're each called to a particular role, and it's important we fill that role and not try to be something we aren't. Each of us has been given a certain amount of gifts, and it's our responsibility to use them. Thérèse was discouraged at reading this, since her passion to serve Jesus was such that she saw herself in every role of the Church.

Then she read on. In Chapter 13, Saint Paul explains that what is central to every gift and role in the Church is love. In this love, she saw her answer.

I understood that Love alone makes its members act, that if this Love were to be extinguished, the Apostles would no longer preach the Gospel, the Martyrs would refuse to shed their blood . . . I understood that *Love* embraces all vocations, that Love is all things, that it embraces all times and all places . . . in a word, that it is eternal!

Then in the excess of my delirious joy, I cried out: "O Jesus, my Love, at last I have found my vocation, my vocation is Love! . . . Yes, I have found my place in the Church, and it is you, O my God, who have given me this place . . . in the heart of the Church, my Mother, I will be Love! . . . Thus I shall be all things: thus my dream shall be realized!!!"

When anyone asked what I wanted to be when I grew up, I used to say that if I could find a job that just paid me to love people, I'd do that. So you can imagine how it felt to meet this Catholic nun who had the same desire.

THE COMMUNION OF SAINTS

Reading *Story of a Soul* opened my eyes to the world of Catholic saints, a subject I knew almost nothing about. Before I read Saint Thérèse's book, I still held the belief that Catholics didn't love Jesus, their faith wasn't genuine, they blindly went through the motions and prayed affectionless prayers. And while for some Catholics that may very well be the case, I've learned that looks can be deceiving. Many Catholics, I came to realize, love Jesus, have a genuine faith, are engaged in each and every motion, and affectionately pray memorized prayers. On the outside, their faith looked much different than what I was used to, but it wasn't any less genuine than my own.

After Saint Thérèse made me question how I viewed

Catholics, I wondered if there was anything else I might be wrong about. I started by learning more about the saints themselves. I'd seen depictions of them on little cards and statues, and knew they were believed to have lived holy lives, but since Catholics seemed to revere them almost like idols, I had steered clear of them. Even if these saints were in heaven, I imagined they would be horrified to learn that people worshipped little statues and cards of them.

I wasn't wrong. The Catholic Church teaches that worship is for God alone, so the saints *would* be upset seeing anyone worship something or someone other than God. But if Catholics aren't worshipping the saints, then what is with all the prayers, cards, and statues? I mean, the saints were growing on me thanks to Saint Thérèse, but until my questions were answered, I was stuck.

What hindered me was my perception of how Catholics interacted with the saints—but I hadn't ever asked one what their relationship to the saints was. So I started polling all my Catholic friends.

The consensus among them (and incidentally the teaching of the Catholic Church and Scripture) was that those who have lived a holy life and are now with Jesus in heaven aren't sitting idly by, twiddling their thumbs. Revelation 8 describes the throne room of God as mingled with the smoke of the incense ever before God, which are the prayers of the saints. Growing up, I'd always read this as being about the prayers of us here on earth, but the passage describes the saints as being there with God. They're worshipping God and praying for those left behind on earth.

I heard what my friends were saying, but I had to put it into a perspective I could better understand. So I started with Saint Thérèse. While she was in her cloistered convent here on earth, she prayed so much for people all over the world that she is considered a patron saint of missionaries. And she told people that after she died she would spend her time in heaven doing good on earth. She saw her work of prayer on earth as just the beginning of the work of prayer she would have in heaven. And not for her own glory, but to help others know God, just like a missionary.

Things were starting to make sense. Asking Saint Thérèse, who was in heaven with Jesus, to pray for me was like asking anyone else to pray for me. She just happened to be in heaven and not sitting next to me at church. But what about the statues of saints, or even of Jesus and Mary? Were people worshipping them? If so, weren't they idols?

That's when I learned that for most Catholics, their devotion to certain saints is akin to the love of a family member who has passed. We may keep a photo of that family member in the house, we may even affectionately kiss it as we recall our relationship to that loved one and how much we miss them. Do we think the photo is actually that person? Of course not! But the photo reminds us of who that person is and what they mean to us. Pictures and statues of saints are the same thing for Catholics, who will often decorate their home, office, car, garden, water bottles, etc., with images of saints who inspire them to be strong in their faith, to be holy, and to live like Jesus.

That explanation hit home. While I never had a photo

hanging in my room of Jim Elliot, I plastered his quotation everywhere. Every time I saw his words, my desire to live my life for Jesus was renewed. I never worshipped Jim Elliot, but he was a constant inspiration to me for years. And not just Jim. Corrie, Amy, and good old Mrs. Duckworth. They all inspired me to grow in my faith. Just like with Jim, I never had a photo of them on my wall, but I carried the stories of their lives with me.

When I eventually decided to end my protest and become Catholic, I had to choose my patron saint—a Catholic saint who inspired me, or whose journey with Christ was similar to my own. I knew that Mary, the mother of Jesus, was someone I wanted to emulate, given my history of admiring her as well as what I'd been learning from her life of sacrifice. But Saint Thérèse had the same overwhelming love for Jesus that I did. I felt I could relate to her more than any other saint I'd learned about. I'm thankful that Father Boyle, the priest who brought me into the Church, allowed me to take both saints as patrons: Mary and Thérèse. And when on the day I became Catholic I was gifted a statue of Saint Thérèse, I gave it an excited and grateful little hug. I look forward to the day when, in heaven, I can give her a real hug and thank her for her prayers and her help on my journey of faith.

CHAPTER 8

How Are Women Viewed
in the Church?

Where do I fit in this puzzle?
What good are these gifts?
Not a martyr or a saint
Scarcely can I struggle through
All that I have ever wanted was to give my best to You
—"DANDELIONS" BY FIVE IRON FRENZY

Be who God meant you to be and you will set the
world on fire.

—SAINT CATHERINE OF SIENA

CALLED TO WHAT?

My favorite job was when I worked as a church janitor.
I had wanted to serve God with my life for as long
as I could remember, and longed to work in a church. In
the Protestant denomination I was raised in, the only roles
I saw women in were missionaries, church secretaries, and
children's ministry directors. Since I was fresh out of high
school I knew I didn't have the experience to be any of

those things, but still my heart yearned to serve full-time in ministry.

I noticed that pastors' wives were pretty involved in ministry, so I started thinking that this would be my "way in" to full-time ministry. I loved youth ministry specifically, so I figured I needed to find a single youth pastor (or someone who wanted to be a youth pastor), fall in love, get married, and then I'd automatically be in ministry! I told my older and married youth pastor about this plan; he chuckled and suggested that I get a new one, because youth pastors were all "jerks." He had a point. I knew several by that time, and while a couple of them were kind, there were a few who had been jerks. I shifted my "marriage" plan to the back burner.

Since working in full-time church ministry seemed outside of my reach for the time being, I focused instead on volunteering all my free time. I spent my days working at a Christian elementary school in a variety of positions, and with the rest of my time I served in the junior high ministry, spent my summers as a camp counselor, was a leader in our college-age ministry, and was involved in our church's musical theater outreach program.

And then it finally happened. I had begun looking for a better-paying job than the one I had at the school, when I learned that my church had a full-time janitorial position open. I couldn't stop thinking about this job—my foot in the door to work in full-time ministry. I applied and was offered the job! I was going to spend my days at church! Sure, I'd be cleaning toilets, but that didn't matter to me. I was finally getting paid to serve Jesus and work for the Church!

I spent my mornings unlocking doors, cleaning bathrooms, vacuuming, and doing other odd jobs at the megachurch I attended. I spent the last part of my day going to each pastor's office and emptying their trash. I had a deep admiration for these men who spent their days serving God with their lives, so getting the chance to serve them in this little way was the highlight of my workday.

As I continued to work at the church, I realized I was going to need more education if I was ever going to do more than janitorial work there. Eventually I felt the Lord calling me away to college. I moved out-of-state and majored in Bible/theology and journalism. I learned in some of my classes that while there were possible church jobs for women, a lot of denominations looked down on women doing ministry . . . including the one I'd been raised in. This came from a couple different passages in the Bible where it could be interpreted that women weren't allowed to speak in church or hold positions of leadership over men.

I had never wanted to be a pastor or anything, but my desire for full-time ministry seemed to be a divisive topic all the same. My heart was increasingly broken as doors seemed to slam in my face. There didn't seem to be a place for me in the Church unless I wanted to do missionary work, children's ministry, or women's ministry. I wasn't too interested in any of them.

I began to let go of my desire to work in a church. After all, I knew that I could still do amazing work for God in other places. After I earned my bachelor's degree, I got a job working as an admissions counselor at my alma mater and set myself about helping others work toward their own dreams of ministry, all while never fully letting go of my own dream to somehow work in full-time church ministry.

I ended up deciding that perhaps becoming a licensed professional counselor might be a good option. I knew some churches that had licensed counselors on staff, so I started working on a master's in counseling. During this time I was hired as a resident director at my alma mater and was reminded that my dreams of ministry weren't about licenses and psychology, but about meeting people where they were and helping them grow in their relationship with God. After getting halfway through my master's in counseling I switched gears, entered seminary, and began working on a degree in pastoral ministry.

Even in 2013, being a woman in seminary was an oddity, especially in the more traditional Protestant denominations. While our school was interdenominational, it still reflected a greater Protestant culture that didn't seem to know where women fit into things. I had female classmates who, like me, had a strong desire to serve God in His church, and who had tried to remain optimistic and positive despite feeling like our place in ministry was questionable and even debatable. I had a couple of women professors I learned from during that time, and I began to wonder again if perhaps my calling wasn't to serve in a church. Maybe I could be a professor instead?

During my final year in seminary, I took a church ministry course: I was the only woman in the class. Thankfully, the male professor was gracious and inviting, I already knew a couple of the guys in the class really well, and the others whom I got to know along the way were great. Toward the end of the semester, we finally got around to the topic of women in ministry. I remember going to class that day feeling uncharacteristically anxious about how this topic would be handled.

I don't recall much of what the professor said, because none of it was new to me. He covered the spectrum of debate about women in church ministry, including the question of whether they could teach men and in what context, and the roles women did have—in children's ministry, youth ministry, and women's ministry. I do recall that the atmosphere in the class felt different than before, and I couldn't help but feel like I was the elephant in the room.

Thankfully, my professor seemed aware of the awkward situation he was in: teaching a woman about women in ministry. To my surprise, when he finished his lecture he asked me if I had anything to say on the topic. All eyes were on me.

I thought back on my experiences and those of other women I knew. I realized this was an opportunity to speak up for myself, and for them, to this group of future pastors. I told the class that for the most part, women who fight to be involved in full-time ministry do so because they feel strongly called and want to serve. Unfortunately, the more they are denied opportunities to serve, the more toxic they can get. I recognized that there was a possible spectrum of opinions in the room on women in ministry, but I asked these men and future pastors to please listen to the women they met in their churches, and help them find a way to minister.

I was glad to have the opportunity to speak up for those of us who felt called to ministry, but I also couldn't help but feel like I was asking for the bare minimum . . . that we at least be heard.

PERCEPTION OF OPPRESSION

The little I knew about women in the Catholic Church made their experience seem on par with my own. I knew they weren't permitted to be priests, which was actually the least of what bothered me. Like I've said, I never had a desire to be a Protestant pastor, so I couldn't care less about being a Catholic priest.

That said, I *was* bothered that priests couldn't be married. Since one of my hopeful plans to be in full-time ministry was to marry a pastor, I was frustrated that Catholic women didn't even have the option at all. And when I learned about the vow of obedience for religious women, my stomach was in knots. I couldn't help but think of all the pastors I'd known, many of whom wouldn't have permitted me to do full-time ministry; and the thought of being subject to them and unable to serve the Lord was a horrible thought. I knew nuns existed, but I wasn't entirely sure how they fit into everything or what kind of life they lived, but I imagined they were just as ignored and oppressed as I was.

A year or so later, when I felt the Lord asking me to look into the Catholic Church for myself, this issue of how women were treated, viewed, and respected was high on my list of things to look into. Thing is, I didn't want to read about it in a book. I wanted to see for myself how women were regarded.

FINALLY HEARD

After I'd been attending Mass for a few months, the priest of the parish, Father Boyle, asked a few of us young adults to meet with him. He intended to start a weekly young adult ministry, and wanted to consult with us about the best way to go about doing that. While I was about the same age as everyone there, I was the only one who wasn't Catholic, and therefore very confused about his invitation.

"Father, I'm not Catholic. Why do you want *my* help with this?" I sheepishly asked.

"Well, you're a young adult who attends Mass at this parish regularly, so I'd like your thoughts. Plus, didn't you study how to do this very thing?"

Surprised, I nodded my head. For the first time in all my years of ministry I felt respected, and my education was seen as valuable. I didn't have to defend what I'd learned or argue about why my voice would be helpful at the table. I was seen and accepted as I was. I began to wonder if perhaps my assumptions about how the Catholic Church viewed women were a bit off.

We eventually started our weekly young adult group. We'd get together for an hour of Eucharistic adoration and confession, followed by snacks, conversation, and games in the rectory basement. Father Boyle claimed to be too old to stay and visit with us, so he put Father Andersen in charge of our fellowship time.

During one of our young adult nights, after we had just sat down with our snacks, Father Andersen came downstairs with a few books in hand and a huge smile on his face. He announced that that evening was the Feast of Saint Teresa of Ávila, and in honor of the occasion he wanted us to talk about her writings—specifically which ones were our favorites. I was the only one in the room who hadn't known it was her feast day, and hadn't read any of her work! Everyone else excitedly grabbed for the books Father Andersen had set on the table so they could find their favorite passages.

In all my years of church ministry, Bible college, and seminary, I had never heard of a woman theologian, let alone one who was revered so highly. Growing up as a Protestant Christian, I'd heard of Beth Moore Bible studies, but those were always for women. I'd heard of certain women speakers as well, but often their theology was siloed into one denomination, rather than being treated as something that could be appreciated by everyone. And I certainly hadn't heard men so interested in any of them that they'd have read their writings, let alone quoted them.

I was in shock. I felt like I was in some sort of dream as Father Andersen, as well as the other guys in the room, quoted from Saint Teresa's book *Interior Castle,* as well as her autobiography. I had no idea that a world existed where female theologians were revered. As we continued the discussion, I learned that Saint Teresa of Ávila, along with Saint Thérèse of Lisieux, Saint Hildegard von Bingen, and Saint Catherine of Siena, were all given the title Doctor of the Church. That title has only been bestowed upon saints whose research and writings have had a significant impact on the theology of the Catholic Church.

Mental vertigo set in as I tried to wrap my mind around everything I was hearing and experiencing. My preconceived notions of how the Catholic Church viewed women were fading away in light of the reality I was experiencing. Women weren't ignored in the Catholic Church, nor pushed aside as only good enough to teach other women and children. No; women were listened to, respected, and even revered.

MARY AND EVE

Why was it that women in ministry seemed to be treated so well in the Catholic Church, in contrast to what I'd seen and experienced in my circles in Protestantism? I mulled this question over until I heard someone refer to the Virgin Mary as "the New Eve."

As a woman born and raised Protestant, there was one thing imprinted on me the minute I heard the Garden of Eden story: Eve screwed it all up. As one of her daughters, this invisible guilt hovered over me like a little rain cloud for most of my life. Through the years, I heard every possible sermon on that fateful piece of fruit: lighthearted jokes, the opinion that Adam should have intervened, and messages that subtly labeled Eve and all of womankind as dangerous.

Eve, along with Adam, made the initial mistake by disobeying God and bringing sin, suffering, pain, and destruction into the world. I learned that the Catholic Church teaches that Adam's sin was in fact even greater than Eve's—because he didn't stop her. But Mary, by obeying God and allowing herself to be part of His plan for salvation, brought Jesus— the New Adam—into the world, to redeem the world.

This realization touched a nerve.

Mary, in her obedience to God, redeemed not only Eve, but all women. And no, I don't mean "redeemed" in the way that Christ redeems. What I mean is, I suddenly knew that it was acceptable to hold my head up *as a woman.* That the original sin may have been committed by the hands of a woman—but so had salvation.

Suddenly my experience in Protestantism made so much sense! Most Protestant churches and denominations have little to do with Mary. We always avoided spending too much time thinking or talking about her, because she was "too Catholic" a topic. But because our theology of Mary was lacking, so was our theology of women! There was a shadow of Eve's sin hanging over my place as a woman in the Protestant Church, but a bright spotlight over my role as a woman in the Catholic Church, because of Mary.

This picture/icon, titled *Mary and Eve,* sums up their relationship. I saw this picture before becoming Catholic and something about it struck a nerve, so I hunted down the original and purchased a copy. It was painted by a Catholic sister, Sister Grace Remington, OCSO, a Cistercian nun at Our Lady of the Mississippi Abbey, in Iowa. Every time I look at it, I feel the dignity of my womanhood being restored. Ah—it's just beautiful!

VEILING THE SACRED

I was beginning to understand the theology of the Catholic Church in regard to women, but I was still skeptical about a few things. For example, I had noticed a few women in the Catholic church I attended wearing head coverings or veils. While I hadn't grown up in a Protestant denomination that practiced women covering their heads, I was aware of the tradition and the Scripture it came from. I even had friends who attended churches where the norm was for all the women to have their heads covered. I was told this had to do with submission to their husbands and to the other men in the church.

Per usual, I translated what I was seeing in the Catholic Church through my own experience with these Protestant churches. However, I learned that what I saw as oppression was quite the opposite. Veils are used in the Catholic Church to cover that which is sacred. For example, in most Catholic churches, the tabernacle where the Eucharist is reserved is often covered with a veil, because what is housed within that golden box is divine. Similarly, because women have the innate ability to bring forth life, whether bodily or spiritually, they are seen as sacred and revered as such.

One evening, I found an abandoned veil lying around after praying vespers with my Catholic friends and decided to put it on as a joke. I walked out of the chapel and laughed while saying, "Surprise! Look at the Protestant girl wearing a veil, everyone!" Sure enough, I got a few laughs, as well as some shocked looks. Father Mark was so amused, he asked if he could snap a photo. I gladly obliged. Little did I know I'd come to love the symbolism and practicality of veils so much that I'd wear them all the time!

ABILITY VS. AUTHORITY

How the Catholic Church viewed women was becoming increasingly clear, but I still had questions. For example, if women were listened to, respected, and even honored, why were there no women in the leadership of the Catholic Church? This one stumped me. So when I overheard someone asking a Catholic nun about her thoughts on the all-male priesthood, my ears perked up and I listened closely.

She explained that she wasn't interested in women becoming priests. Women had the physical ability to do the job, but they didn't have the authority.

Her summary was simple and got me thinking. I had always focused on the physical and even emotional tasks of being a priest, but I hadn't ever considered the idea of authority, nor the idea that authority is given to certain individuals and not to others.

I continued to ask questions.

What I learned is that Jesus didn't skip over women being priests because they were less-than, which was where my mind had immediately gone. Christ didn't give them that authority, because He had a different job in mind for them, one that complemented the job He gave to men.

The roles of both men and women in the Church are relational, interacting with each other to demonstrate the relationship God has with His people. In the Catholic Church, a priest isn't just someone who ministers to the people; he is meant to act in the person of Christ himself.

This is most properly seen in his ministry during Mass, but, by his ordination to Holy Orders, he is also meant to be a sign of Christ in all he does. The weight of this role is one the priest should always have in his mind when he ministers to the Church. Likewise, men who aren't priests are meant to act in the person of Christ in their family.

Okay, now before you come at me with the pitchforks because it seems like Catholic women are in a vulnerable position, let me explain their important role. Women represent the Bride of Christ, the Church. The Catholic Church is actually referred to as feminine for this reason, and is even called "our Mother."

So if men are meant to represent Christ, and women are meant to represent the Church, what does that relationship look like? Saint Paul explains this in the letter he wrote to the Ephesians. You can see how he goes back and forth between talking about men and women in a marriage, but he is also referring to the Church. This passage has been abused by men who distort God's Word for their own power and gain, but when you read the whole text, you see that there shouldn't be abuse when it's lived out completely—only a relationship of love and sacrifice:

Be subordinate to one another out of reverence for Christ. Wives should be subordinate to their husbands as to the Lord. For the husband is head of his wife just as Christ is head of the church, he himself the savior of the body. As the church is subordinate to Christ, so wives should be subordinate to their husbands in everything.

Husbands, love your wives, even as Christ loved the church and handed himself over for her to sanctify her, cleansing her by the bath of water with the word, that he might present to himself the church in splendor, without spot or wrinkle or any such thing, that she might be holy and without blemish. So [also] husbands should love their wives as their own bodies. He who loves his wife loves himself. For no one hates his own flesh but rather nourishes and cherishes it, even as Christ does the church, because we are members of his body. "For this reason a man shall leave [his] father and [his] mother and be joined to his wife, and the two shall become one flesh." This is a great mystery, but I speak in reference to Christ and the church. In any case, each one of you should love his wife as himself, and the wife should respect her husband. (Ephesians 5:21–22, NABRE)

This passage may say that women are to be subject to their husbands, but it's because men are supposed to treat women as well as they treat their own bodies, to cherish them, and even to sacrifice themselves for them. Not only is this true for men and their wives, but for priests and the Church. By living this life of sacrifice, men are supposed to demonstrate with their lives the ultimate love and sacrifice of Christ for all of humanity.

This passage says a lot about the role of priests and husbands, but what about women as the Church?

In order to understand the role of women, we need to understand the role of the Church, since it becomes the mirror of our role. The Church is called to respond to the sacrifice of Jesus by spreading the good news of the Gospel, to educate and nurture new believers, and bring forth life in the Church.

When Christ calls us to something, He does so knowing that it's not only part of who He created us to be, but that it will also be a challenge. Both roles are vital, and both require sacrifice. Jesus sacrifices himself for the Church, whose response is to sacrifice herself in order to bring forth life. If a priest or a husband is doing his job in caring for the Church or his wife, then the life that is brought forth is not something forced but a natural response to their sacrificial act of love.

Of course, what I'm talking about is what we are all called to. This is the standard, and it's not hard to see that we fall short of this standard. Men in every role struggle to love their wives sacrificially. Women in every role struggle to sacrifice themselves for life. The standard our society sets forth for both men and women, however, is to base your life choices on yourself and what will bring you the most happiness and pleasure. Unfortunately, this means that sacrifice of any kind isn't on the menu.

The world is repulsed when it looks at how the Church views the relationship between men and women, because it directly contradicts the norm of self-love. Even men and women who claim to live pious lives can fall into this trap of self-love. When this happens, even the beautiful self-giving standard that Christ has demonstrated becomes distorted and destructive. A single bad marriage doesn't demonstrate that marriage in general is wrong any more than a broken-down car proves that cars are bad.

All of this took years of learning, listening, and heaps of reflection for me to understand. I had a lot of my own baggage to sort through before I could clearly differentiate between the standard Christ set and the distorted images I'd seen and experienced. Just because I'd only ever known broken-down cars didn't mean well-running cars didn't exist.

CALLED TO BE

Through all the years I felt called to serve God in the Church, I could never seem to figure out what role I was supposed to be filling based on what I saw in my own churches, in college, and even in seminary. I found myself resonating with the lines I quoted at the beginning of the chapter: "Where do I fit in this puzzle? / What good are these gifts? / Not a martyr or a saint / Scarcely can I struggle through / All that I have ever wanted was to give my best to You."

Even in that quotation was a glimpse of the answer. It was upon encountering the way the Church views men and women that the pieces came together, and I began to see my place in the puzzle. I was never called to a specific role or job, but to be a certain kind of person in the Church: a life-giving woman.

To be a woman in the Catholic Church is not to fit a

stereotype. I've known lots of life-giving women, and none of them were quite the same. Some have been nerdy tomboys like myself, others fit a more traditional understanding of femininity; some were strong leaders, while others were meek and quiet. There is beauty in our variety, because we all have different gifts in our ability to bring forth life.

I recently had a conversation with a grandmother at my parish. She was lamenting that she had a hard time relating to the interests of her grandchildren, but she noticed that I was able to relate to their generation. I understood their interests in anime, superheroes, YouTube, and old-school cartoons, and got their quirky sense of humor. While I could relate to the playful and worldly side of her grandkids, she was able to bring them stability, history, and unconditional love. This grandmother and I are both living out our roles in the Church, bringing forth life by being who God created each of us to be; and, in so doing, we are both able to set the world on fire.

CHAPTER 9

What Is Religious Life?

FIRST ENCOUNTERS

Sister Helen Moore, of the Sisters of the Holy Names of Jesus and Mary (SNJM), was the first religious sister I ever met. The year was 2004, and I was working on a writing assignment for my college journalism class in which we were to interview and write a story about a group of people we knew little about. I wasn't Catholic, but I had been fascinated by Catholic nuns and sisters since I saw the movie *Sister Act* ten years earlier. I didn't ponder for long which group I was going to be writing about.

After being greeted at the convent door, I was led into a front sitting room and waited for Sister Helen to join me. Being a journalist in training, I decided to take notes on the room, especially the TV in the corner with a stack of DVDs in the cabinet underneath. Curiosity took over and I nervously got off the loveseat where I'd been sitting and looked through these sisters' movies. I was pleased to discover both *Sister Act* and *The Sound of Music,* but then quickly returned to my seat. I'd never met a nun, and I was nervous I'd be caught sneaking a peak at their DVD collection.

When Sister Helen came into the room I was surprised to see someone who looked like your average grandma: short gray hair, modest and simple "normal" clothes instead of a habit. I asked her my list of questions and listened as she talked about community life, the sisters' ministries, and her love of art. She gave me a tour of their convent, and even showed me their small but beautiful chapel on the second floor. Before leaving, I even bought a couple of her hand-painted greeting cards.

My first experience with sisters had been pleasant, but nothing like what I'd seen in the movies. I may have had all my prepared questions answered, but I left feeling even more confused about what being a religious sister was all about.

Eleven years later, on Saturday, November 21, 2015—the day before I was received into the Catholic Church—I found myself on the threshold of another convent. My friend Sara suggested I join her on a visit with the Franciscan Sisters of the Eucharist, who lived just twenty-five minutes outside of Portland, Oregon, in a small town called Bridal Veil. They were having a work day, where folks from around the area would come and help the sisters with chores on their large forested property.

The sisters lived in an old Italian-style villa that had been abandoned and left in disarray before they'd purchased the property in the mid-1970s. Thanks to their hard work and the efforts of friends and neighbors, you'd never have known that this villa-turned-convent had ever been home to snakes, rats, and an assortment of other wild animals.

We were ushered into their large kitchen and offered coffee and some pastries. The sisters all wore simple brown habits with a brown rope cincture belt adorned with three knots. Each of them had short hair with a sheer black veil crowning the top of her head and flowing down to the middle of her back. After our little breakfast and a quick prayer, each of the volunteers was given their chore assignments for the day: I would be helping Sister Jacinta clean out the chicken coop.

I'll never forget the cheerful demeanor of Sister Jacinta as we chatted away while shoveling pounds of hay, bark, and chicken poop, nor the penetrating smell of that chicken poop and how it lingered with me long after I left the convent that day. But what stayed with me longer than that smell was the overwhelming peace and joy I felt as we worked. I couldn't stop smiling, and I even broke into laughter several times over how happy I was doing something so disgusting.

It wasn't the chore itself that brought me so much joy, but the environment I was doing the chore in. I was at a convent with Catholic nuns in habits, and I couldn't shake how at home I felt with them, or the feeling that I was getting a glimpse into a future the Lord was leading me into. After all, the next day I was going to be received into the Catholic Church and the biggest question I'd had for God during my whole journey into the Church was: "Since I'm becoming Catholic, does that mean I'm also going to become a nun?"

WHAT IS RELIGIOUS LIFE?

Perhaps you grew up around nuns and sisters and had the experience of seeing these mysteriously matching madams regularly at school, church, or the hospital. Or you're like me, and the closest you got to religious women was weekly episodes of *The Flying Nun* with Sally Field or a yearly rewatch of *The Sound of Music* with Julie Andrews.

Either way, everyone seems to have a feeling of curiosity when they encounter a nun. There's something intriguing about a group of women who live together, dress alike, and have vowed to never get married. Their life is baffling—and the fancier the habit or the more cloistered and hidden away the community, the greater the intrigue.

"Religious life" describes the lives lived by nuns, monks, sisters, and brothers, and these groups of people are collectively referred to as "religious." While each of these groups of religious will have different ways of living, there are a few things they all share in common. They usually live in a community that shares a mission (known as an "apostolate"), a culture (known as a "charism"), and a unique spirituality that's often based on the spiritual teachings of a particular saint or group of saints. Additionally, these religious all make the same three vows before becoming a permanent member of their respective community: the vows of poverty, chastity, and obedience.

But when did people start living this esoteric way of life, and why, in our modern society, do people still want to be religious?

A SIMPLE BEGINNING, LEADING TO A FAITHFUL FUTURE

Christian men and women have been living out their faith in countercultural ways since the very beginning of Christianity. They would often remain single and commit themselves to a life of prayer and service to the Church. One of the earliest recorded examples of Christians living this type of life is Saint Anthony of the Desert, also known as Saint Anthony the Great, who is called the father of monasticism and lived around the year 300.

Saint Anthony's journey into a monastic way of life began when he and his sister lost their parents. They had a sizable inheritance that would have continued to provide for their needs, but Saint Anthony felt compelled to follow the words of Christ in Matthew 19:21: "Jesus said to him, 'If you wish to be perfect, go, sell what you have and give to [the] poor, and you will have treasure in heaven. Then come, follow me'" (NABRE). Saint Anthony eventually sold their property and possessions and gave the money to the poor. He went to live in the desert to spend his days in prayer, while his sister went to live with a community of

Christian virgins, which is the earliest reference we have to a community of women like this.

Shortly after Saint Anthony died in 356, (not-yet-Saint) Augustine of Hippo, an intelligent and worldly man, had a profound and life-changing conversion. He withdrew from his prominent place in society to live a life of prayer with a small group of companions. Until this point, if men entered into a life of prayer they did so in solitude, but Augustine chose to gather in community with others who had a similar desire for a life of prayer. He wrote a basic list of guidelines for how to live this new life in the context of a community, known today as the Rule of Saint Augustine. Those who have followed this rule through the centuries are known as Augustinians.

Saint Augustine also had a sister, Saint Perpetua of Hippo, who not only lived in a community of consecrated virgins similar to Saint Anthony the Great's sister, but ended up being the superior of that community. Saint Augustine shared his rule of life with this group of women, and even helped them with some internal conflicts after the death of his sister.

This life of prayer within a community became more widely received with the arrival of Saint Benedict about fifty years later. He wrote an even more comprehensive rule of life than Saint Augustine had, and he also went on to found twelve monastic communities that followed this rule. This was the beginning of the religious order known as the Benedictines.

Saint Benedict also had a sister, Saint Scholastica, who

wanted to live a life of prayer in community and, just like Saint Perpetua, adopted her brother's rule and adapted it to a community of women. In doing so, she founded the female order of Benedictines.

This way of living a life of prayer in community continued to grow and develop, adding a number of different orders along the way. Up until the 1200s, the men and women who lived in these orders were cloistered, which means they remained confined to their monasteries and convents. That began to change with orders like the Franciscans and the Dominicans, whose ministries involved going out and preaching.

The main purpose of each new order was still centered on a life of prayer, but each of these new orders also tried to meet specific needs they saw in the Church or in the community. For example, in the year 1610, Saint Francis de Sales and Saint Jane Frances de Chantal founded the first non-cloistered order of nuns who would go out into the community to care for the sick and the poor. This order, known as the Congregation of the Visitation, was also unique in that it accepted older, widowed, and sickly women into the community.

The introduction of this new way of doing religious life ended up having a huge impact on new orders, as well as on previously established orders. This impact included a new distinction between women who lived in a cloistered community (nuns) and those who would leave the convent to minister to those in the community (sisters).

As the refinement of religious life continued, the wearing of habits became more common. The habit is a reminder to the sisters of their charism and spirituality, while also acting as a sign to others of the order and the consecrated nature of the sisters' lives. That's why you can see sisters in brown, gray, blue, black, white, and even red habits—each one representing a unique order and way of life.

In the 1960s, after the close of the Second Vatican Council, religious orders were encouraged to get back to the roots of why they were founded and to figure out how to live out those ancient ideals in a modern way. This led to many orders, like the one Sister Helen was in, letting go of their habits to wear "regular" clothes. The desire was to seem more approachable and less outdated. Some orders, like the Franciscan Sisters of the Eucharist, chose to still wear a habit but updated it to a modern rendition of a historical Franciscan look. Other orders felt that continuing to wear the habit, as-is, was in keeping with their roots and would even aid in their modern ministry.

The entrance process was also refined over time in order to help interested women discern if religious life was really what God was calling them into. The process for most orders now is from five to nine years before a sister makes a vow to remain a sister for the rest of her life. The hope is that the sister-to-be has plenty of time to discover that she is not called to religious life before she makes any permanent vows. As you'll continue to see, there are a lot of challenges in living life as a religious, so it's important for those who feel called to be able to enter in and see if they can live the life, but also to allow for a long process so that those who come to realize it's not for them are free to leave before they would be breaking any vows.

THE THREE VOWS OF RELIGIOUS LIFE

Two months before I entered the Catholic Church, I sat down to talk with Father Boyle, my parish priest: I couldn't get the idea of becoming a sister out of my head. I imagined myself in a full habit, going around helping people, and being married to Jesus, my life being full of constant joy. At this point, I hadn't met the Franciscan sisters yet or had any experience with sisters other than Sister Helen. But still, I couldn't stop dreaming of religious life.

Father Boyle listened patiently as I told him how I'd always admired sisters, how much I loved Jesus, and that I was convinced God was calling me to be a sister.

"Well," he chuckled, "let's get you Catholic first."

I laughed as well. After all, I knew that I was jumping the gun. Thankfully, he didn't write me off, but instead asked me a very important question.

"You know that sisters take vows of poverty, chastity, and obedience; how do you feel about those?"

I had known about their vows, but I hadn't thought too deeply about what they meant. I explained that I'd always valued and practiced chastity in my life, so I felt good in that area; and that I grew up poor, so I knew all about poverty. I visibly grimaced when I got to obedience, though. I didn't want to lie to him, but I also didn't want to give the impression that I was horrible at being obedient. I hesitantly told him that I wasn't great at obedience . . . but that I was working on it.

As much as certain aspects of religious life have changed with the passage of time, the vows of poverty, chastity, and obedience have remained consistent. These three vows are what the Catholic Church calls the evangelical counsels. They aren't a requirement for salvation, but because they are based on the teachings of Jesus (Matthew 19:10–12, 19:21; Mark 10:17–22; Luke 18:18–23) they can be adapted to all walks of life, and are therefore counsels for all Christians, showing the best way to grow in perfection in this life.

POVERTY

Every monk, nun, and sister takes a vow of poverty, though how they live it out varies depending on which religious order they belong to and what their rule of life states. For example, the Franciscan order was founded by Saint Francis in 1209 with an emphasis on living a radical and extreme form of poverty. They were to own nothing at all, and to rely on the handouts of others for their basic needs.

In 2016, I was able to go on pilgrimage to Italy, and when we stopped in Assisi I got to see the level of poverty that Francis preached about. Housed in a display case in the crypt of the Basilica of Saint Clare, the first female Franciscan, were the habits of both Saint Francis and Saint Clare. I was struck by the rough and patchworked fabric—a sharp contrast to the crisp and clean habits of modern sisters. I imagined what it would be like to wear this sort of habit and felt a pit in my stomach. These two founders' habits humbled me and taught me my first lesson in poverty.

Living a life of poverty isn't only about material possessions and wealth. Often, an excess of money, the latest technology, collectables, nice cars, and all the latest and newest versions of things can act as a distraction from what is most important. For example, wearing a habit every day—whether threadbare or neat and tidy—keeps a religious from being distracted by concerns with their own appearance, or with having the latest fashion.

Another way to see this is through possessions. I've known a few religious communities that don't allow community members to have personal possessions, meaning that what they bring into the community becomes a shared possession of the community. That book, table, chair, board game, etc. is no longer "yours," it's "ours." The idea is the same for things like technology. Computers, phones, iPads, etc., are all owned by the community and given to each member according to their need. For example, I use a phone that is shared by the community in order to post my videos on TikTok, and I am using a shared laptop to write this book.

CHASTITY

The automatic assumption most people make when they hear the word "chastity" is that it's referring to an abstinence from sex; but to strive for a life of chastity goes far beyond the avoidance of a simple physical act. For example, you can have a chaste marriage. While rare, this could mean it's a marriage where the couple has agreed not to have sex with each other. However, more commonly, a chaste marriage is one in which the couple refrains from having sex with anyone else but their spouse—and also avoids even "little" temptations that might lead to an emotional or physical interest in anyone other than their spouse. In other words, chastity in marriage is not just a physical devotion, but a wholehearted devotion to your spouse. By this meaning of the word "chaste," there are probably a lot of couples out there that have chaste marriages, even if they don't know there is a term for it!

Chastity in religious life is the same: exercising wholehearted devotion to one's spouse. But in the case of a religious, their spouse is Jesus himself. So a religious not only vows to refrain from having sex with anyone, but even just thinking about romantic attachments is to be avoided. There are often specific rules set up in religious communities to help guard oneself from falling into temptation.

But chastity in religious life goes beyond abstaining from sexual and romantic attachments. Chastity involves how you treat other people as well. Oftentimes in our culture, relationships can be more self-indulgent than self-giving. We all want to feel loved, to feel seen, to be wanted and needed, and so we seek out relationships, both romantic and platonic, to try and fill those needs. However, love involves sacrifice and giving of oneself. If we are focused only on using others to meet our own needs, then we aren't truly loving anyone but ourselves. So to have a chaste love for others means not seeing people as a means to an end, but learning to love them selflessly, whether they can do anything for us or not.

Parents understand this sort of love on a very deep level. When children are babies they are in need of everything: food, clothing, shelter, supervision, nurturing, education, and love. However, a baby can't do anything to meet the needs of its parents, and the parents would be remiss if they tried to use their child to meet their own needs. To be a parent is to live a life of sacrifice for another human being. This is often why those in religious life are described as spiritual fathers and mothers. If a religious is truly living a chaste life, then they are focused on meeting the needs of those they minister to, and not using them to meet their own selfish needs.

OBEDIENCE

When I first learned about the vow of obedience, every fiber of my being hated the mere thought of it. I saw obedience as a form of subjugation and an abuse of power. I couldn't wrap my mind around why someone would voluntarily submit to someone else. And I assume that most of you reading this probably see it the same way. Obedience requires trust, and the older we get the harder it can be to trust others. And if you have any unresolved trauma involving an abuse of trust, then a vow of obedience can even become a trigger. Despite my concerns, I knew God was calling me to religious life, and I would have to face my fear of obedience.

Thankfully, I'd spent years working through any trust issues I had with God. That's right, you can have trust issues with God! In fact, I'd say that nearly everyone does. But how do you heal trust issues with God? Well, the same way you do with any other relationship: It takes time and getting to know someone better. I had always loved God, but because of the pain and trauma in my past I had a hard time trusting Him. However, as I've gotten to know who He really is, I've started to trust Him more. Some levels of trust were easily achieved, and others were extremely difficult. Becoming Catholic was the biggest leap of faith I'd taken with God, and He proved himself trustworthy over and over again in that process. So when I was ready for religious life I knew that, since God was leading me into it, even with all its difficulties, I could trust that He knew what He was doing. That said, trusting God seemed easy compared to trusting people.

In our humanity we have a great capacity for doing good to others or doing harm to them . . . and sometimes it happens that we hurt others even if we don't mean to! I see that capacity in myself, so of course I know others can do the same. But in religious life we are meant not only to trust our superiors, but to *obey* them. So how do you obey a broken and sinful human being, knowing that they may break your trust or hurt you, even if unintentionally? You learn to trust God more than mankind.

You can get an idea of what obedience looks like in the movie *The Bells of St. Mary's.* Bing Crosby plays Father O'Malley, a priest sent to oversee a Catholic school run by a group of religious sisters. The headmistress, Sister Mary Benedict, played wonderfully by Ingrid Bergman, is constantly butting heads with Father O'Malley on how to run the school. Sister Benedict has poured her heart and soul into the children and feels that Father O'Malley isn't running the school the way he should.

Over the course of the school year, it is discovered that Sister Benedict is very ill. The doctor insists she be sent away to heal, but that she not be told about the illness, as it could cause her to despair and thereby hinder her healing. When Father O'Malley tells Sister Benedict that she is going to be transferred once the school year is over, you can see the look of pain in her eyes as she processes the news, and then her quiet resolve to practice obedience and accept this change. Even by the end of the movie, as she's about to leave the school she loves so dearly, we see her on her knees in the chapel. However, she isn't asking for the situation to change, but for her heart to change and to see God's will in all things.

She is upset with Father O'Malley—there's no doubt about that—but in her prayer we see that her trust isn't in this priest but in God's will. God is the object of her faith, and that's why her faith fuels her resolve. This may be a movie, but I can attest to walking through similarly painful moments of internal wrestling due to a decision I'm asked to obey. I wish I could say I've walked through each moment with the poise and dignity displayed in Ingrid Bergman's portrayal of Sister Benedict, but I have experienced the change of heart that she prays for—because my ultimate trust is not in my superiors, but in God.

Now, to be transparent, obedience is not only difficult for those under the obligation to obey, it's also difficult for those dishing out the orders. The Rule of Saint Augustine has a strict directive for superiors to this effect:

> The superior, for his part, must not think himself fortunate in his exercise of authority but in his role as one serving you in love. In your eyes he shall hold the first place among you by the dignity of his office, but in fear before God he shall be as the least among you. He must show himself as an example of good works toward all. "Let him admonish the unruly, cheer the fainthearted, support the weak, and be patient toward all" (1 Thes 5:14). Let him uphold discipline while instilling fear. And though both are necessary, he should strive to be loved by you rather than feared, ever mindful that he must give an account of you to God. (Chapter VII)

In *The Bells of St. Mary's,* Father O'Malley is challenged by the doctor to do what is best for Sister Benedict even if it means she may hate him. He's challenged in his ability to love her in true charity by doing what is best for her at a cost to himself. This movie shows what obedience done well can look like, on the part of both the religious and the superior.

There are, of course, superiors of orders who have fallen

into the temptation to wield their authority in unhealthy, selfish, or destructive ways. Some fall into this temptation rarely, while others seem to lead without a second thought to the pain they cause others. Just because someone is a religious does not mean they are perfect. Which is why Saint Augustine reminds the superior that they need to always remember they will one day give an account to God for how they led those in their charge.

Whether the challenges faced in religious life come from a superior, another member of the community, or the challenges of living a life devoted to the love and service of others, the vows a religious makes are a double-edged sword bringing both pain and growth. With great pain often comes even greater beauty. Those religious who have died and gone on to become saints can serve as inspiration for what it looks like not only to live out one's vows as a religious, but to follow the evangelical counsels we are all called to.

COMMUNITY LIFE

A unique and vital aspect of religious life is the life of the community. I didn't just feel called to serve the Lord with my life; if that had been the case, I could have easily served God while remaining single or even being married. A call to religious life is also a call to a life of community.

A couple years ago I asked a religious brother what the best part of religious life was, and what the worst part was.

His answer was simple: "The community." He explained that the people you live in community with can be your biggest support and your greatest challenge. I heard a sister once say that a community of sisters is a miracle in and of itself, since it consists of a bunch of women living together under the same roof and not killing each other.

The life of a religious community is difficult to describe. The best way to describe it would be to say it functions much like a family. In a women's order you have a mother superior who has the responsibility of care for the entire community. You have younger sisters who often take on the more physically demanding tasks with the strength of their youth, while the older sisters perform the housework. And when a sister is no longer able to "pull her weight" in the community, she is cared for by the community.

There are sisters you get along with and sisters you laugh with. There are also sisters who challenge you and sisters who rub you the wrong way. However, at the end of the day, you know you're all in this beautiful life of ministry together, all working toward the same goal of becoming more like Christ.

I love movies like *Sister Act* because they show the variety of the types of sisters you can find in a convent, as well as the love and devotion sisters have for each other—despite whatever disagreements they may have between them. At the end of the day, they are a community.

MY OWN JOURNEY

Ten years have passed since my "I wanna be a sister" meeting with Father Boyle. The hardest part of the journey was taking that first step to visit a convent; not as a casual volunteer helping out, but as a woman interested in possibly joining and living the life. I had envisioned a basic story in my head: I'd visit a few convents, find the right one for me, go through the process of selling my things and quitting my job, and then I'd enter religious life and live my dream.

With all I've learned from a lifetime of following Jesus on the crazy adventures He has sent me on, I should have known my experience would be anything but simple and straightforward. All the experiences I was having—all the convents I visited, religious I met, and research I did—were for religious life, but not because He was leading me into an already established order. He had something else in mind.

In 2018, I met with a group of seminarians, men studying to become priests, who also couldn't shake the feeling that they were being called into religious life. We talked about the value of religious life, love of the liturgy, heart to serve and teach people, desire for community life, and the central importance of the Eucharist. They shared with me their desire to establish a new religious order for men, and invited me to pray about joining them by founding a new religious order for women that would be a mirror of their own community. Initially I thought they were crazy, but after our meeting the Lord impressed on me that this was the direction He wanted me to go. I felt like Saint Clare, the first female Franciscan, who followed after Saint Francis and his religious brothers, with the intention to found a new religious order.

Founding a religious order is not for the faint of heart. Our journey has been challenging, fraught with pain and difficulty—but it has also been the most beautiful and amazing experience of my life. We have seen the Lord open doors and provide for us in ways I could never have imagined, and He has led us to places we didn't even know existed. The first step of founding a new order is living the life, and the Lord has provided us with the place and opportunity to do just that. The men live in a small monastery, while I live in an old convent, and in the midst of our life of prayer we teach at a Catholic school, help out at local parishes, serve at the Mass, lead youth groups, teach people about their faith, lead outreaches for the poor in the area, run a Catholic radio station as well as a thrift store and coffee shop, host retreats, have an online ministry, and run a small farm.

When I felt God calling me into religious life, I had discerned with a couple of orders and felt worn out at the end of each day. I asked the Lord how I could live this life He was calling me to if I couldn't seem to make it through a short visit. His reply was simple: "If I called you to it, I'll give you the strength to do it." That list of all our ministries, coupled with our ability to keep up with them, is a constant testament to me that He has truly called us to this life.

At the heart of my desire for religious life, all I ever wanted was to live in such a way that I could spend my days loving people and loving Jesus. And that's what I do. Really, that's what all religious do, whether they are in habits or not, out in public or not, famous or not; they all strive to love Jesus and love others. Which happens to be what we're all called to do anyway.

CHAPTER 10

What Does Faith Look Like in Real Life?

Thou hast formed us for Thyself, and our hearts are restless till they find rest in Thee.

—SAINT AUGUSTINE, Confessions

WHERE TO BEGIN?

I was overzealous about my first Lent as a Catholic. During Lent, the season of preparation leading up to Holy Week and Easter, Catholics take on a voluntary sacrifice that will remind them of the suffering of Christ and spur them on to more prayer. I had dabbled with Lenten sacrifices before becoming Catholic and was amazed at how much the discipline increased my focus and prayer life, so I had high expectations for my first official Catholic Lenten season.

Not only did I have three things I wanted to give up for Lent, but there were also another five disciplines I wanted to incorporate into my life. I think I managed to do them all the first two days of Lent, but when my ideals collided with real life, I found myself burning out and eventually failing to do anything I'd planned.

Around this time, one of the priests I knew asked me how my Lent was going. I relayed to him my idealistic nosedive and the apathy that had set in. He nodded along as he listened intently. He wasn't surprised by anything I told him. He said new Catholics are often overzealous in their spiritual practice, and that the danger in taking things to one extreme is the possible swing the other way when we don't live up to our own expectations. As excited as we are, we need to keep new spiritual practices simple and attainable.

That Lenten lesson is true for all of us. Maybe our motivation to grow spiritually is too ambitious: We've had a taste of truth and beauty, or perhaps had an amazing or even miraculous experience. Either way, we want heaven, and we want it now. Anything less isn't enough. The problem is, if our sights are set too high, we may lose steam if it seems the journey is taking too long. Living a life of faith isn't a sprint, it's a marathon.

Perhaps zeal isn't our problem though. We may be kept from moving forward because we have a certain expectation we aren't meeting. We may think we're supposed to be at a certain level spiritually, and since we aren't there, we give up without ever trying to move forward.

Saint Thérèse had this issue. She would hear stories about the saints and get discouraged because she didn't think that level of faith was attainable for her. Thankfully, she eventually realized that God wasn't calling her to be a saint overnight! That's true for us all as well. To move forward in faith, we need to know where we're at and what our first steps will look like.

Years ago I decided to participate in an Avon Walk for Breast Cancer; a 39.3-mile walk over the course of two days. If that sounds overwhelming, you are correct. In fact, I failed horribly. I didn't take my training seriously. My pride told me I was great at walking and would be fine. I walked eighteen miles the first day and only five miles the following day; I finished 16.3 miles short of my goal.

Thankfully, I had a friend who was determined to help me finish that walk. She encouraged me to sign up with her and try again. This time, I was disciplined in my training. I had a personal trainer, set a walking schedule, and I kept to that schedule rain or shine. By the time I got to the walk, not only was I able to walk 26.2 miles the first day, but I was able to get up the second day and finish the final 13.1 miles: 39.3 miles in total.

Each of us is faced with our own spiritual marathon. Some are longer than others, but nothing more is being asked of us than to take it one step at a time.

FAITH AND PRAYER

Prayer is an important first step in your journey whether you're a beginner in the faith or a veteran. A journey of faith is first and foremost a relationship with God, so it's important to build on that relationship wherever it is in the process, and the number one way to do that is prayer.

Never talked to God before? It's not as complicated as you might think. He's always listening, so all we have to do is speak: Say hello, tell Him how you feel about talking to

Him, tell Him what you're struggling with, thank Him for the blessings in your life. In the words of Saint Jane Frances de Chantal, "Follow your own way of speaking to our Lord, sincerely, lovingly, confidently and simply, as your heart dictates." It's just as simple as that.

And for those of you who are further along on your journey, don't forget the simplicity of a conversation with God. The busyness of life can cause us to get stuck in a rut with any relationship, and how we interact with God is the same. Sometimes when my life gets super busy I make sure to intentionally set aside some time to just talk to God about what's going on in my life—how I'm feeling about everything, what I'm stressed about, and what I need help with. I also make sure there's time for silence. He doesn't always respond, but if I'm always the one talking I'll never be ready for when He does.

FAITH AND TRUST

As we grow in our relationship with God, as with most relationships, we may run into an obstacle that prevents us from going further until it's addressed. Trust can be a difficult aspect of our human relationships, and how much more so with God! That's not to say that He isn't trustworthy, but our life experiences may try to convince us otherwise.

I learned this lesson during a trip to Hawaii with some friends. One of them, Cory, was playing tour guide. Cory had grown up on the island of Kauai and seemed to know every tree, river, and beach as he showed us around. We went on many hikes, and I saw views that were so breathtakingly unreal, they brought tears to my eyes.

Some of the hikes seemed to offer more adventure than beauty, and a few were borderline dangerous. However, even the more rugged and treacherous trails were made easy with Cory's help. He'd show us where to walk, and even where to step. I recall on one hike the way forward led us down a steep and muddy path alongside a river. I became overwhelmed trying to figure out how to navigate exposed tree roots and thick mud without losing my balance and sliding all the way down. Cory saw my hesitancy and stepped in to offer his help.

He told me to follow in his exact footsteps, and when the way was too rough he'd turn to offer me his hand. As I focused on following his every move, I found myself reflecting on my relationship with God and how He'd led me through difficult times in the same way Cory was leading me down this treacherous hill: one step at a time. Sure enough, we made it down the hill without either of us falling! I turned to look back at the path we'd taken, and it was only then I was able to see the beauty that surrounded me during that stressful journey!

I was able to have that experience because I trusted Cory. I knew he knew the island well from living there, and that he wasn't going to play a prank or lead me into a worse situation than I was already in. I knew Cory had my safety in mind and would help me get down the hill—and he did!

What about our relationship with God? How much do we trust Him? If He offers us a hand, are we willing to take it or do we pull back and try to do things on our own? I can think of many seasons when God reached out a hand, but I ignored it and decided to do things on my own. Trauma, abuse, neglect, betrayal, and rejection by others can lead us to lose trust not only in people, but in God as well. But the thing we always need to remember is that God is nothing like people. Think of the most loving, forgiving, and sacrificial person you've ever known. Perhaps you haven't known any and have only heard about people who are like that. Either way: God is even more loving, forgiving, and sacrificial.

But it takes time to build trust after there's been a history of broken trust . . . and that's even more true of our relationship with God. So on your journey it's important to reflect on how much you trust Him—or how much you don't trust Him. It's also important not to beat yourself up for your lack of trust or assume that He's mad at you for it. He knows better than anyone why you're hesitant, and the healing that will need to take place for you to grow in your trust of Him. Thankfully, He's also more patient than anyone you've ever known.

FAITH IN REAL LIFE: TRUTH, BEAUTY, AND GOODNESS

Those who seek God usually fall into one of three categories. They are drawn either to His truth, His beauty, or His goodness. These transcendent realities go against the lies, ugliness, and evil that exist in each of our lives and reveal that there is something more to life than our common experience. You could even ask yourself right now: Why did you pick up a book that's about God? What makes you desire to venture forward on a journey of faith? Wherever you are in your life, and whatever is drawing you on this journey, it's helpful to know what is so enticing about each of these aspects of God, and what they tell us about Him.

BEAUTY

I've always loved and appreciated nature, and often feel humbled by the sheer vastness of a noisy ocean, the grandeur of a quiet forest-filled mountain, or even the simplicity of a windy desert or prairie. Each environment awakens all my senses and makes me aware of my own humanity, but each also speaks to the intentionality of a master artist. In a sense, all art is just imitation of Creation itself—every painting, for instance, tries to capture the beauty rendered by the original artist. There are even elements of nature in architecture, mathematics, graphic design, music, etc. Each medium reflects a deeper beauty that is found in Creation.

I spent a lot of time with the Franciscan Sisters of the Eucharist after becoming Catholic. They have a beautiful convent located in the Columbia River Gorge. Nestled against a cliff in a moss-covered forest, with a waterfall and river running through their property, the sisters are able to educate visitors on the beauty of nature and the many ways it speaks about its Creator.

I got into the habit of visiting their property once a

month for their work days. While on my first visit I helped clean out the chicken coop, on subsequent visits I picked up fallen branches, fished leaves out of rivers and ponds, weeded rose gardens, and trimmed ferns and trees. I had never been a fan of gardening or outdoor work, but the Franciscan Sisters taught me to look beyond the physical activity and see the beauty of Creation and the truth it spoke about its Creator.

This was a bit of a foreign concept initially. I recall staring at some leaves and trying to figure out what they were trying to tell me. Ha! Thankfully, I eventually understood what these sisters were talking about shortly after they taught me how to prune an apple tree.

I had a small group of apple trees in my backyard at home, but their fruit was all bland, so I'd let the squirrels enjoy them. Then, on one of the work days, I was asked to help clean up the branches that were being pruned from the sisters' apple trees. I listened with interest as one of the sisters trained another volunteer on which branches to cut and where, so that the tree would produce more delicious fruit.

I hadn't realized you could trim a tree to change the flavor of its fruit! The sister explained that if the tree wasn't trimmed, then its strength would be stretched thin among all the branches; but if you trimmed it back, it could concentrate its nutrients in the remaining branches. Excited about this new lesson, I waited until the next best season for trimming, found some pruning tools in the garage, and climbed a ladder to the apple trees in my backyard as I thought about how delicious the apples would be that next harvest season.

As I worked to prune back the countless branches that had sprung up after years of neglect, I started reflecting on my life. I had been feeling more stressed and anxious, teetering on burnout. I was busy with my position at work. I was active in my parish and would often be at the church for daily mass and parish events. I was also active in the other Catholic churches in the area, going to different events and special masses.

In addition, I was running a house of Christian women (both Protestants and Catholics). I was discerning religious life, so I was also trying to spend as much time with the Franciscan Sisters as I could. On top of that, I was fitting in time with family and friends.

I didn't have any room left to take care of myself.

I had gained weight, and knew I needed to change things up so I could eat healthier and get exercise—but I had no idea how to fit that in.

With each branch I cut, I realized I had a lot in common with these apple trees. I had too many branches in my life. I was spreading myself thin and was unable to take care of myself and my health in the process. I stopped trimming and stared at the tree I was pruning, which seemed to be teaching me a lesson about the origin of stress and anxiety in my own life. Tears welled up in my eyes; I needed to trim some of my own branches before my own fruit lost its flavor and wasn't any good to anyone.

The sisters had told me that God can use nature to teach us about life, but I had no idea the lesson would be so deep and challenging. I'd been looking for some sort of ethereal lesson on God and the universe, but instead God was using nature to give me practical advice I could apply to my life. I just needed to jump in, get my hands dirty, spend some time with nature, and listen.

TRUTH

In the movie *The Wizard of Oz,* there's a famous scene where Dorothy is standing face-to-face with the infamous wizard. He is shown as a large floating head surrounded by fire, clouds of smoke, and lightning. Before granting her request, he sends Dorothy on a wild-goose chase to collect the broom of the Wicked Witch of the West.

When Dorothy accomplishes this task and returns, the wizard begins to gaslight her into thinking there's more that she has to do before he can help her. Only then does her faithful dog Toto sniff out the real wizard who is hiding in a little room and controlling the larger-than-life fake. Still attempting to maintain his charade, he utters the famous words "Pay no attention to that man behind the curtain."

Anyone who has been gaslit will tell you that it can make you feel like you're going crazy, because you no longer know what is true. Our world is full of men behind the curtain telling lies, and all of us need a Toto who can pull back the curtain and point out what's real and what is counterfeit. Truth, even if painful when discovered, is refreshing.

I wrestled with truth a lot in my spiritual journey. The "truth" I'd been raised with was that the Catholic Church was full of lies. I was so convinced of the lies inherent in the theology of the Church that I was afraid to research it for myself.

I reached a point where I couldn't deny that Jesus was leading me to learn more about Catholicism, but I was anxious about cracking open the Catechism and seeing for myself what it said.

I had struggled with fear and anxiety my entire life, and they were like shadows keeping me in chains and away from what is beautiful, good, and true.

I finally read the Catechism of the Catholic Church while on a retreat with the Protestant university I worked for. I was nervous not only to read it for myself but that someone might discover that I was reading it, so I hid it in another book. Taking a deep breath, I read the first page and was dumbstruck. I already agreed with everything it said! As I continued to read I found it resolving theological debates, and even revealing the grandness of God's love. In short, reading the Catechism was refreshing. While reading, I felt like I had stepped out of the noise of the world and was faced with the peacefulness of Truth itself.

GOODNESS

True goodness seems rare in this world. People often assume that no one would do something purely for the good of another. Famous people who perform acts of altruism are often accused of doing so in order to gain positive public opinion and "likes." However, when we see goodness in this world, we are getting another glimpse of the truth about who God is.

This was a concept I learned through the media, of all things.

As I got to know Jesus over the years by reading about Him, learning about Him, and talking to Him, I grew accustomed to the sound of His voice and what was most important to Him. He is Love in its purest expression. He died for all of us—not when we were at our best or because we'd done anything deserving of His sacrifice, but simply because He loved us and wanted to save us from a life apart from Him and His love. I find the goodness of Jesus's love is so intense and beyond our experience that we can never fully understand it in this life.

But that doesn't mean there aren't echoes and imitations of it all around us. Similar to the beauty of nature made evident in an artist's work, this ultimate goodness of Christ is echoed in stories. Music, movies, TV shows, cartoons, books, poems, and even some of the oldest tales passed from one generation to the next attempt to capture this sacrificial love.

One of my favorite examples is in Sam Raimi's 2004 movie *Spider-Man 2.* In the movie, Peter Parker is struggling in his personal life because of his work as Spider-Man, which in turn causes his superpowers to diminish. (Sounds like he needs to prune an apple tree . . .) The local newspaper even accuses him of being a menace and a criminal. Because of all this, he takes a somewhat short-lived break from the superhero life until he has to step in to save the day.

As the villain, Doctor Octopus, fights with Spider-Man on top of a train full of passengers, he decides to speed up the train and cut the brakes. Spider-Man jumps to the front of the train and pushes himself to the breaking point to stop the train, even while a passenger jeers at him from inside. Articles have been written about the beauty and emotional impact of this scene, in which he gives everything of himself to keep the passengers from death. The goodness evident in this famous scene is an artistic representation of the truth of Christ's sacrifice for us.

And this is only one of so many. I've seen glimpses of Christ's sacrificial love for us in *The Notebook, Moulin Rouge!, Guardians of the Galaxy Vol. 2,* the *Lord of the Rings* trilogy, *Armageddon, Terminator 2, Man on Fire, Star Trek II: The Wrath of Khan, Doctor Who, Stranger Things, Avengers: Endgame, Les Misérables,* and animes like *Naruto, My Hero Academia,* and *One Piece.* The goodness of this type of love is told and retold in countless ways.

The more you understand who Jesus is, the more you realize the love He has for us is etched into our hearts and you see it everywhere. He is pure Goodness and Love. We seem to either long for this kind of love or run from it, but either way we continue to repeat the tale of a love so strong that the lover is willing to sacrifice everything.

TAKING THE LEAP

It's one thing to read about taking a leap of faith, but it's another thing to do it. The question is, will you take that first step? I've always been the kind of person that likes to plan all my moves out in advance and research all the possible scenarios and dangers that lie ahead, so that I can have plans and backup plans. The temptation for me has always been to learn just enough about something that I convince myself I don't have to step outside of my comfort zone and actually take that next step. I've nearly fallen into that temptation in all of the major decisions in my life—even when looking into Religious Life! But at some point, I had to make the choice to move away from plans and into the actual experience.

What will your choice be? Are you going to seek after Truth, Beauty, and Goodness? Are you going to get to know your Creator? Are you going to talk to that Catholic friend you've misunderstood? Are you going to learn to trust God? Perhaps you're Catholic and need to go back to confession or mass. Or perhaps there's something else the Lord was pointing out to you as you read this book. As much as I've been writing these words, this whole book was God's idea in the first place, so I can only imagine He's been trying to reach out to those of you reading along.

Whatever decision you make, know that you're in my prayers. As one who has taken several leaps of faith, I know how scary and unsettling they can be. I've always said that life with the Lord is one adventure after another. So, what adventure is He leading you on? And are you willing to take His hand?

ACKNOWLEDGMENTS

The thanks I have for the many people in my life who have encouraged, supported, challenged, listened to, inspired, and loved me is endless. I am grateful to you all. I am especially grateful to Becky Nesbitt for seeing a book hiding inside this TikTok Nun, to Chris Park for helping me navigate the book-writing process, and to Matthew Burdette for helping me refine my thoughts and ideas. To those who walked with me on my journey into the Catholic Church—whether named or unnamed in these pages— thank you for your help, companionship, and patience. To all my followers on TikTok, your questions inspired what is written here. And to my religious family of brothers in the League of the Blessed Sacrament, thank you for always having my back.

ABOUT THE AUTHOR

Sister Lisa Hezmalhalch lives in the White Mountains of eastern Arizona, where she is founding a religious order of Catholic sisters with a love for the liturgy, Latin, farm life, serving others, and education. A passion for sharing the overlooked gifts found in Catholicism and dispelling the misconceptions about the Church brought her to TikTok, where she's known for the silly and the sincere.

Instagram: @sisterlisah
TikTok: @sisterlisah